JOE MONTANA

By Marc Appleman

A *SPORTS ILLUSTRATED FOR KIDS* BOOK

First Edition

Library of Congress Cataloging-in-Publication Data
Marc Appleman
    Joe Montana /Marc Appleman — 1st ed.
        p.   cm.
    "A Sports illustrated for kids book."
    Summary: A biography of the man who may be the greatest football quarterback ever to play the game.
    ISBN 0-316-04870-4
    1. Montana, Joe, 1956 — Juvenile literature. 2. Football players — United States — Biography — Juvenile Literature. 3. Quarterback (Football) — Biography — Juvenile Literature.
    [1. Montana, Joe, 1956- 2. Football players.] I. Title.
    GV939.M59A67 1991
    796.332092 — dc20   91-14760

Sports Illustrated For Kids Books is an imprint of Little, Brown and Company.

10 9 8 7 6 5 4 3 2 1

SEM

For further information regarding this title, write to Little, Brown and Company, 34 Beacon Street, Boston, MA 02108

Published simultaneously in Canada by Little, Brown & Company (Canada) Limited

Printed in the United States of America

Written by Marc Appleman
Cover photograph by Paul Jasienski
Cover design by Pegi Goodman
Comic strip illustrations by Brad Hamann
Interior line art by Jane Davila
Produced by Angel Entertainment, Inc.

Contents

1

The Comeback Kid

With 3:10 left to play in the 1989 Super Bowl, many people in the standing-room-only crowd at Miami's Joe Robbie Stadium felt the game was over. The San Francisco 49ers were trailing the Cincinnati Bengals 16-13, and they had the ball on their own eight-yard line. The end zone was 92 long yards away.

On the Cincinnati sideline, a young player turned to veteran Bengals wide receiver Cris Collinsworth and smiled confidently. "We got 'em now," he said. Cris wasn't so confident. He asked, "Have you taken a look at who's quarterbacking the 49ers?"

Cris Collinsworth had good reason for concern. The

game might have seemed in the bag if the Bengals had been playing any other team. But the Bengals were facing the 49ers — and Joe Montana. And Joe wasn't called the Comeback Kid for nothing.

Last minute heroics were nothing new for Joe Montana. He had led the 49ers, his college at Notre Dame, and even his Pennsylvania high school team to a total of 33 fourth-quarter comebacks!

So the prospect of covering 92 yards in just over three minutes didn't phase Joe. If he needed a burst of confidence, he could have thought back to the 1982 NFC championship game, when he connected with receiver Dwight Clark for a touchdown pass with less than a minute to play to beat the Dallas Cowboys. Or to the 1979 Cotton Bowl against the University of Houston, when Joe left a sickbed to lead Notre Dame back from a 34-12 deficit to victory, and finished off with a TD pass in the final two seconds of the game. Or to his high school all-star game back home in Pennsylvania, when he led his state team to the winning touchdown over the Ohio all-stars with only 2:12 left to play. But Joe didn't need to remember.

By calling two plays at a time in the huddle, Joe quickly

attacked the Bengals' defense and marched the 49ers down the field. Quarterbacks generally call only one play at a time, but Joe was trying to save precious time for his team. But more important, he was preventing the defense from setting up properly for the 49ers offense.

Joe completed eight of nine passes in an 11-play drive that covered 92 yards, finally hitting wide receiver John Taylor on a 10-yard touchdown pass with just 34 seconds left in the game. The 49ers won 20-16. Those 11 plays would go down in football history as The Drive. It was one of the most exciting Super Bowl finishes ever.

"Montana is not human," Cris Collinsworth said after the game, shaking his head in amazement. "I don't want to call him a god, but he's definitely somewhere in between. I have never seen a guy that every single time he's had the chips down, he comes back."

Joe's teammates had come to expect such miracles from their quarterback. "When you see Joe do it in the clutch as much as we have, you think he can do it every time," said 49ers offensive tackle Bubba Paris.

The 49ers wide receiver Jerry Rice had a great game, catching 11 passes for 215 yards, but he was very humble when he accepted the award as the game's Most Valuable Player. "I did okay," he said of his performance. "If it was up to me, I would have given the MVP to Joe."

With Joe's spectacular performance and the praise from teammates and opponents alike, it's hard to believe that he had been fighting for his job as a starting quarterback just two years earlier. But at the end of the 1987 season, after the 49ers had put together a 13-2 record in the regular season only to be upset in the first round of the playoffs by the Minnesota Vikings, Joe's career in San Francisco seemed in jeopardy. Joe had suffered through a serious back injury in 1986 and all kinds of smaller injuries in 1987. He was 31 years old then and had played nine tough years in the NFL, which is considered a long career. Even though he had led the 49ers to two Super Bowls in the previous five years, the 49ers owner and coaches were beginning to wonder if Joe still had what it takes. They even considered trading him during the off-season.

When the 1988 season began, Joe found himself sharing the starting quarterback job with his former backup, Steve Young. Joe's confidence was deflated and he wondered about his future. He didn't know where he stood.

It seemed like a repeat of what he experienced growing up, when he had to overcome the doubts of a high school coach who said he was too frail and a college coach who didn't understand or appreciate how special Joe's talents were.

But Joe came fighting back. And when he got his chance, late in the '88 season with the 49ers in danger of not making the playoffs, Joe showed that he still had the magic touch. He led the 49ers not only into the playoffs, but to a dramatic Super Bowl victory over the Bengals.

Joe was unstoppable after that. The next season he quarterbacked the 49ers to a 14-2 record and a blowout over the Denver Broncos in Super Bowl XXIV. In 1990 he led San Francisco to another 14-2 record and to within one game of a third straight Super Bowl appearance.

Many consider Joe Montana the best quarterback ever to play the game. And with the way he has started off the 1990's, he can only get better. But this determined small town boy from Monongahela, Pennsylvania had to overcome great odds to reach that distinction.

2

A Quarterback's Best Friend

Joseph C. Montana, Junior was born on June 11, 1956, in New Eagle, Pennsylvania. He was the only child of Joseph and Theresa Montana. Mr. and Mrs. Montana were both descendants of Italian immigrants who had joined with people from other European countries to settle Western Pennsylvania. These immigrants made the area famous for four things: coal mines, steel mills, farms, and quarterbacks.

Johnny Unitas, the former Baltimore Colts great who is in the Professional Football Hall of Fame in Canton, Ohio, is from Pittsburgh, which is 30 miles from Monongahela, the town in which Joe Montana grew up. So is Dan Marino, the Miami Dolphins all-pro quarterback. Johnny Lujack, the former Heisman Trophy winner from Notre Dame, is from nearby Connellsville. Terry Hanratty, who went on to star at Notre Dame and was Joe Montana's idol when he was growing up, is from Butler. Joe Namath, a Hall of Famer who led the New York Jets to an upset victory over the Colts in the 1969 Super Bowl, is from Beaver Falls. Jim Kelly of the Buffalo Bills is from East Brady. All of these towns are within a 40-mile radius of each other.

What is it about the western part of Pennsylvania that produces top quarterbacks? Johnny Unitas claims it is: "Toughness, dedication, hard work, and competitiveness; a no-nonsense, blue-collar background." Joe Namath says because he and the others grew up surrounded by mines, mills, and farms, "Sports became an arena of escape for all of us. I'm not sure what characteristics we all developed, but leadership and an aggressive style were important."

Joe Montana, Senior, of course, couldn't have known that his newborn son would some day become the most famous person on that list of Western Pennsylvania quarterbacks, but back in 1956, he certainly could dream about it.

Mr. Montana himself had played baseball, basketball,

and football in the Navy. He wanted his son to have the opportunity to be a more successful athlete than he was. As soon as Joe was old enough to walk, his father showed him how to throw a ball. Not long after that, Joe could be found standing with a bat and ball in his hands while he waited for his dad to come home from work for lunch.

When Joe was 3 years old, Mr. Montana changed his career so that he could spend more time playing ball with his son. He quit his job as a telephone equipment installer for Western Electric because that job required him to spend too much time away from home. Instead, he went to work in an office for the Civic Finance Company of Monongahela. Joe had friends who were his own age, but it was his father who taught him to play and love sports.

"Sometimes you look at a kid and you know he's a natural," Mr. Montana says of his son. "It didn't take much to encourage him. It seems that Joe was interested in playing with a ball all his life."

Joe's dad was always there to help support his son's strong athletic interests. Joe spent many afternoons after elementary school, sitting on the front steps of his family's two-story frame house waiting for his dad to return home from work. Even when Mr. Montana was dead tired from a hard day in the office, he would drop his briefcase and pick up a baseball glove to catch Joe's pitches, or take off his suit jacket and run after one of Joe's football passes.

From the time Joe was a kid, there was no question that he was being groomed to be a quarterback. The natural athletes in Monongahela became quarterbacks. It was a Western Pennsylvania tradition. But few father-and-son combinations worked at it so hard.

The Montanas asked permission to use the yard of one of their neighbors as a practice field. The Polonolises had a tire swing that Joe senior would move back and forth while Joe tried to throw the football through the center of the tire. It was an excellent drill to help develop passing accuracy. After that drill, father and son would return to their own yard. Joe senior would run pass patterns or snap the ball from center and work with Joe on setting up to throw properly. After the drills were completed, Joe and his dad would play catch and chat about what they did that day.

"I wanted to make sure he got the right fundamentals," Mr. Montana says. Joe's father had read books about quarterbacking and studied pro quarterbacks on television.

He knew how important proper footwork was to the success of a passer, and he wanted to pass that along to Joe. "You watch some quarterbacks, sometimes they need two steps to get away from the line of scrimmage," he explains. "I felt the first step should be straight back, not to the side. We worked on techniques, sprint out, run right, run left, pivot, and throw the ball."

Some friends and neighbors felt that perhaps Joe senior was pushing his son too hard. Mr. Montana disagrees. "It's just that he loved it so much, and I loved watching him," he says. "And I wanted to make sure he learned the right way."

Joe himself says that the motivation to play has always come from inside of him, not from being pushed by his father. He simply loved to play. "The game has always been so challenging to me, that it has stood alone as my motivation to stay with the sport as long as I have," he says.

But even with all the hard work, Mr. Montana understood that it was most important that sports be fun for his son. There were many times when father and son, on their way home, would stop in an alley between their house and the Polonolis house for a catch. Or, they would go to the basketball court and play one-on-one. Nothing was planned.

If the two of them were together, it was just likely that they would start playing ball. "We had an all-sports relationship and didn't talk about much of anything else," Joe writes in his autobiography, *Audibles*. (An audible is the term used to describe when a quarterback changes the play at the line of scrimmage because of something he sees in the defense. This is something Joe would become very skilled at.)

Joe began playing organized sports when he joined the Monongahela Little Wildcats peewee football team at the age of 8 years old. The rules said you had to be at least 9 years old to play, but Mr. Montana wanted his son to play so much that he lied about his age.

From the start, Joe was a natural. He had the physical tools and a sharp mind suited to making quick decisions. Plus, all the instruction time and practicing he had done with his dad gave him an advantage over the other kids. Joe just knew by instinct what to do on the football field without even having to think about it. And, he had that Western Pennsylvania-bred toughness and will-to-win.

"We ran a pro offense, with a lot of the stuff he's doing now, the underneath stuff," says Carl Crawley, Joe's coach on the Little Wildcats. He is referring to how a pro quarterback must "read" a defense to see which defensive players are covering which offensive players before he decides whether to throw or run with the football.

"Joe would roll out," Coach Crawley continues. "If the cornerback came off, he'd dump it off; if he stayed back, he'd keep going and pick up five or six yards. He was an amazingly accurate passer for a kid."

Joe was a star, but his teammates didn't resent him. Like many other kids who don't have any brothers or sisters, he was shy and quiet around strangers, but he was friendly with kids once he got to know them. Even as an 8-year-old playing with older kids, Joe was confident in his ability and he let his play on the football field serve as his calling card.

"There was no show-off in him," Coach Crawley says. "He wanted to win, and he'd do whatever it took, and that's another thing the kids liked about him. With Joe on the field, they knew they were never out of any game."

Joe played a lot of football, but he loved all sports. During the spring, Joe played baseball. As a pitcher in Little League, he threw three perfect games. Basketball was his favorite sport, though, because everyone on the court was involved. He also used the quickness he had developed on the football field. He loved the dodging and faking, and the challenge of trying to beat the man guarding him.

There was no organized basketball program for young kids in Monongahela so Mr. Montana came up with a solution. When Joe reached fourth grade, Mr. Montana got together a group of fourth-graders and formed 10 different teams, each with its own uniforms. He also rented a gym in a local armory five nights a week, and he paid the janitor to clean up after practices. The kids chipped in a dollar each to help out.

With Joe senior and other fathers serving as coaches, the kids were drilled on the fundamentals of the game. Later on, during Joe's junior high years, Mr. Montana would set up an all-star team of 10 players who traveled to midget basketball tournaments throughout the region. Joe would be the star guard on the team.

Those were fun days for Joe, but by the time he was 10 years old, he was beginning to feel burned out on sports. He was playing a different sport each season and he wanted to do other things. "When I saw kids involved in non-sports activities," he writes in his autobiography, "I was a little jealous. I wanted to get off the field."

What Joe really wanted to do was quit playing football and join the Cub Scouts. He was particularly tired of practicing. Joe liked practicing basketball, but he didn't enjoy the drills and repetitions involved in practicing football.

Joe's football team had been practicing for a few weeks when Joe decided that he would approach his dad to discuss quitting the team. Joe knew Mr. Montana wouldn't be happy about his decision and he wasn't looking forward to bringing up the subject. He recalls their discussion in *Audibles*.

"Dad, I want to quit football, I'm tired of it," Joe said. "I want to join the Cub Scouts."

"Go ahead and quit," Mr. Montana said.

Joe was stunned by his dad's initial reaction. But the more Mr. Montana thought about it, the more determined he became that his son was not going to leave the team now that practice had started. Quitting was one decision that Mr. Montana would not accept from his son. One day Joe senior approached Joe and said: "Get your [football] stuff on."

Joe said, "You said I could quit!"

Mr. Montana was just getting started. "I don't believe you should quit, and I was wrong in telling you that you could quit," he said. "If you want to quit, you can. But only after you finish playing out the year. I don't want you ever to quit anything you've already started."

As it turned out, there would be no Cub Scouts for Joe. He finished that football season and the following season. And the following season. And the following season. . . .

Joe says that his dad encouraged him, rather than pushed him, and he feels fortunate to have had such a father. But Joe also understands that what his dad did might have been for himself as much as it was for Joe.

"I never asked him, but he is so sportsminded that he might be living his dream, his sports fantasy, through me," Joe writes in his autobiography. "Because this may be true, I always think about Mom and Dad whenever I step on the field."

When Joe won the second of his four Super Bowl rings, he gave his first Super Bowl ring to his dad. It was his way of saying thank you to a father who was also his best friend.

3

Ringgold High

By the time Joe entered Monongahela Ringgold High School in 1970, he was already becoming a local hero. In addition to starring in football, baseball, and basketball at Finleyville Junior High, he had once high-jumped 6'9", and had set a junior high school record in his only attempt at throwing the discus.

His friends called him Joey. He was tall for his age, and quite skinny, with a mop of yellow hair on his head. By the time he was a sophomore, he had shot up to 6 feet, 165 pounds. He may have looked awkward, but he could sure play — and win at just about anything he tried.

Joe went out for the varsity football team. It was

something he had been looking forward to ever since he had thrown spirals through the tire in his neighbors' backyard.

High school football games on Friday night were a big event in Monongahela. Ringgold High did not always have a winning team when Joe was growing up, but the team started turning around soon after Coach Chuck Abramski became head coach. By the time Joe got there, the Ringgold Rams were an up-and-coming team among the schools that played Pennsylvania Class AAA football. Class AAA football was the highest level of high school football in the state.

Joe had expected to join the team and quickly become starting quarterback. After all, he had been the star quarterback of his pee wee and junior high school teams. Coach Abramski knew all about that, but he had his own idea of the type of player he wanted to play quarterback on his team, and skinny Joey Montana was not that guy. Coach Abramski even started calling Joe "Joe Banana," a nickname that Joe's teammates began calling him by, too. The coach not only thought that Joe was too thin, but also too young to survive the battles of Class AAA football. It would take Coach Abramski a while to see how special Joe's natural talents were, so Joe sat on the bench all season.

During the summer before Joe's junior year, Coach Abramski told Joe to be sure to take part in the twice-a-week weight-lifting program that he was conducting for all of his players. It was Coach Abramski's way of developing very tough players. But Joe and a number of his teammates did not want to take part in the weight lifting program. After all, Joe never really liked practice, and weight lifting sounded even worse. Why spend time lifting weights, thought Joe, when you could be playing other sports?

Coach Abramski was not used to being challenged. An intense man, Coach Abramski was a perfectionist. He felt that no matter how natural an athlete Joe was, Joe could be even better if he worked harder and if he lifted weights. Then he would become stronger and tougher, and be just the type of quarterback Coach Abramski wanted for his team.

When Joe's junior season began, Coach Abramski did not play him, even though he knew Joe could throw the ball and run with it well in practice. The starting quarterback was 6'3", 215 pound Paul Timko, who also played defensive end. Paul could run the option play, in which the quarterback runs the ball around the end of the line of scrimmage and has the option of pitching back to one of the running backs if it looks as if he'll be tackled. But Paul couldn't really throw the ball.

When Joe did get his chance to play quarterback in practice, it was because Coach Abramski wanted to teach him a lesson. At those times, Paul would move to defensive end. "The coach kept yelling, 'Hit Joe, you'll toughen him up,'" Paul recalls. "So we did that. It turned into a fiasco. Joe didn't like it at all."

"Every day he just beat the heck out of me," Joe says. "I'd be dead when I came home. Football wasn't much fun at that point."

Mr. Montana was also getting frustrated with his son's coach. Joe's father attended most of Joe's practices and all of the team's games. He knew what Joe could do and he saw how hurt Joe was from not getting the chance to play.

Sometimes, adults get into arguments about kids' games, and Coach Abramski's decision not to play Joe angered Mr. Montana. For his part, Coach Abramski, like most coaches, did not like to have parents looking over his shoulder. At one point, Mr. Montana, who had already changed jobs once before to spend more time playing sports with Joe, applied for a job in Pittsburgh. He was willing to move the family so that Joe could enroll at another school.

But Mr. Montana didn't get the job, and the Montanas didn't move. In the 1972 season opener, Joe was there on the bench when the Ringgold Rams were beaten by Elizabeth Forward High School, 34-6. The Rams won the next two games by forfeit because of a teacher's strike, but they lost the two exhibition games that were played in their place. Finally, with a big away game coming up against Monessen High, Coach Abramski decided he had no choice but to change quarterbacks. Joe was going to make his first high school start!

The scene at Monessen was wild. Monessen was the best team in the Big Ten league in which Ringgold also played, and Monessen and Ringgold had a fierce local rivalry. The crowd was screaming as 120 Monessen players came down in single file from the top of their stadium.

This would be a scary start for any new quarterback, but even at this early point in his football career, Joe Montana was Joe Cool. He completed 12 of 22 passes for 223 yards and four touchdowns, three of them were to Paul Timko, who had moved to tight end. Monessen scored a touchdown in the final moments to salvage a 34-34 tie, but for Joe and the Ringgold Rams, it was a victory for their morale.

With Joe at quarterback, the Rams went 4-3-2 that season. Joe was quite adept at running the option play that Coach Abramski liked to run. But now Coach Abramski could also see what a talented passer Joe was, too. Both Joe and Coach Abramski were willing to admit that perhaps they each could give in a little and help the other one out, and by doing so, help themselves. Joe found that there were things Coach Abramski and his staff could teach him. For example, with the help of Ringgold quarterback coach Jeff Petrucci, Joe learned to throw the football on the run.

"Ringgold High's offense had me throwing on the move, and it became second nature to me," Joe writes in his autobiography. "When people talk about my style, they mention my ability to find a receiver and hit him when I'm on the run. Well, it all started in high school."

Joe continued to develop his great instincts for the game. Sportswriters and broadcasters are always amazed at how few times Joe gets sacked by defensive linemen. Even when defenders break through the protective pocket that his offensive linemen form around him, he is somehow able to scramble free. Joe calls that "feeling the color," and says it started in high school.

"Feeling the color is how I'm able to tell when I'm getting pressured in the pocket," Joe says in *Audibles*. "When the defense puts on a strong rush I see the [jersey] colors. I only see colors, not faces, helmets, arms, or legs. Just the wall. Things register automatically. I move out of the pocket fast when that happens."

Joe went on to learn so much about football while he was at Ringgold, that even though he often disagreed with Coach Abramski, he felt he was lucky to have played for him. "He screamed, cursed, and badgered his players, but he always cared about us and our future," Joe writes in *Audibles*. "He cared about me and helped me become a fundamentally sound player."

It was a great time to be 16 years old and Joey Montana. Now 6'2", Joe was a guard/forward on the basketball team who could dunk the ball with two hands from a standing start. He helped lead the Ringgold basketball team to a league title his junior year. Joe averaged 11 points a game. Ringgold played in the state high school tournament and went all the way to the championship game, when Joe fouled out in a 56-49 overtime loss to General Braddock High.

But it wasn't only on the field and the court that Joe was successful. Even though he spent a lot more time playing ball than he did studying, Joe was able to maintain a B average in school. Joe's success on the field coupled with his modesty and good nature helped make him popular off the field. He became so popular that his classmates elected him class vice president in his senior year. He was even dating one of the prettiest girls in town. While most of his friends were hanging out at the popular Eat 'n Park restaurant, Joe spent his time with Kim Moses, who was a cheerleader at Monongahela Valley Catholic High.

Joe had gone from frustration and disappointment as a sophomore in high school to sitting on top of the world as a junior. And then things got even better. During his senior season at Ringgold, Joe led the football team to the Western Pennsylvania Interscholastic Athletic League Class AAA playoffs with an 8-2 record. He was named a high school All-American by *Parade* magazine.

Many college coaches and scouts began attending Joe's games to watch him play. They all hoped that Joe would be interested in playing football for their school. Joe visited the

University of Georgia, Boston College, Minnesota, Penn State, and Pittsburgh. He even received a basketball scholarship offer from North Carolina State. But there was never any doubt about which school was his first choice. Joe senior wanted Joe to go to Notre Dame, and so did Joe. Notre Dame was where Terry Hanratty, Joe's idol, had played. Notre Dame wanted Joe, too. And they offered him a football scholarship.

But there was one more sport that was interested in Joe. After the basketball season, Joe was invited to take part in a major league baseball tryout camp being held in Connellsville. Then, out of roughly 100 prospects, Joe was one of 11 players selected by the scouts to attend a second tryout camp. Mr. Montana thought Joe should attend the camp. After all, if Joe didn't make it in football or if he got injured, Joe senior wanted his son to have other options.

But Joe decided not to go to the camp. After all, one of his dreams was about to come true. Joe was going to Notre Dame to play football.

4

Joe College

When 18-year-old Joe arrived in South Bend, Indiana, to play football for Notre Dame, it didn't take him long to discover that trying to play football for a powerhouse team like the Fighting Irish was very different from being the star quarterback at Ringgold High. Notre Dame has a legendary football program, and its team had won the national championship the year before Joe arrived on campus. Here, Joe was just one of many great players, almost all of whom had been the stars of their high school teams. And he was just one of 11 talented quarterbacks!

Joe also had some difficult adjustments to make off the field. He was away from home for the first time and he found that life on his own was a lot harder and lonelier than it had been at home. Joe was so lonely that he called his dad three or four times a week and frequently made the eight-hour drive from South Bend to Monongahela.

Of course, Joe's father didn't want him to be unhappy. He kept telling Joe to be patient and to stay confident. Sometimes Mr. Montana would drive to South Bend just to watch Joe scrimmage and to bolster his spirits.

There was a good reason why Joe needed to have his spirits bolstered. When he had accepted a scholarship to Notre Dame, he thought that being a part of the Fighting Irish athletic program would be very exciting. And eventually it would be, but not during his freshman year. Notre Dame had a separate, junior varsity team for freshmen. And even in the freshman games, Joe played only briefly.

"I was pretty low on the totem pole, and by the time they reached me I only got to play a couple of minutes," Joe says in his autobiography, *Audibles*. "Psychologically, things were really tough for me. I had never sat on the bench, but worse than that, we had to go to the varsity games. I had to walk into a stadium full of people and couldn't even dress for the game. A few weeks of doing that was enough for me.

I walked out of one game and began to cry."

In his freshman season, Joe ran into problems with his coaches and their attitude toward him. The coaches seemed to feel he wasn't working hard enough in practice, so they were concerned that he wouldn't work hard in games. They wanted their players to be as intense in workouts as they would be on the field. "Joe just wasn't a practice player," said former Notre Dame teammate Steve Orsini. "And that was a big liability in a place where coaches were looking for talent in practices before they'd put it on the field."

Joe also liked to make wisecracks to his teammates on the field, and particularly in the huddle. He did this to keep the players loose. But coaches misunderstood his attitude and thought that he didn't take football seriously enough. One thing that Joe had always been serious about was football, but he had a hard time convincing his coaches of that.

While Joe was struggling with people's attitudes about him on the field, his life off the field improved. He married Kim Moses, his high school girlfriend, during the second semester of his freshman year. This changed Joe's life at college dramatically because he no longer lived in a dorm with roommates. In the brief period in which he had lived on campus, Joe and his roommates played sports in the hall and played practical jokes. They would put a trash can full of water on top of the door to a room so that the next person who opened the door would get soaked. Now, he was a married man with serious responsibilities.

Joe and Kim moved into an apartment off-campus, and Kim got a job as a secretary in the Notre Dame sports information office. Joe spent a lot of time visiting Kim at her office when he had the time between classes, before practices, and on Sundays. Sundays were the the busiest days for Kim because that is the day the sports information departments give the press the information on all the sporting events that take place on Saturday. On Sundays, Joe usually brought along the family dog, Pupper, to visit Kim.

Another major change took place after the football season. Notre Dame coach Ara Parseghian, who is considered to be one of the greatest college coaches ever, resigned because of health reasons. The new coach was Dan Devine, who had coached the Green Bay Packers in the National Football League. Although Joe had been recruited by Coach Parseghian, he hadn't received the kind of attention he had hoped for. Maybe, Joe thought, things would work out better for him with a new coach.

When Coach Devine arrived on campus, Joe was the seventh quarterback on the Notre Dame depth chart. That meant there were six quarterbacks who were considered to be better than he was. In spring practice during Joe's freshman year (college football teams practice in the spring before breaking for the summer), with Coach Devine at the helm, Joe did very well and moved quickly up the chart.

But one good spring practice didn't turn Joe into a star. He still had a lot of work to do to convince his coach that he belonged at the top of the chart. And it turned out that he had a lot of work to do in the classroom as well.

As a sophomore, Joe had a very difficult time academically. Notre Dame is a very good school, and Joe was being challenged in the classroom in a way he had never been challenged in high school. Trying to balance schoolwork, football, and marriage made it even tougher for Joe to maintain his grades. Joe was placed on academic probation, which meant that he had to improve his grades, or he wouldn't be eligible to play football. So even though Joe was trying to become Notre Dame's starting quarterback, he was forced to spend more time studying his books than studying game films, which is how football players learn what mistakes they have made and what strengths their opponents will have.

At the same time that Joe was learning to be both a student and an athlete at Notre Dame, he was also feeling more independent than he had ever felt before. Now that he was married and had his own apartment, and now that his work was clearly cut out for him at Notre Dame, he found it was less urgent for him to go home on weekends to see his parents. But Joe would later remark that you can outgrow your hometown, but you can never outgrow your family.

Going into his sophomore season, Joe felt that he had a good chance to become the team's starting quarterback. But Coach Devine had other plans. The 1975 season began with Rick Slager as the starting quarterback. Rick was injured during the third game of the season, however, and it was Joe who was called off the bench. Joe took over the team in the first quarter with Notre Dame trailing Northwestern, 7-0. He directed the Irish to a 31-7 win!

Joe's father came to most of the games, and he was there to see Joe's great performance. After the game, Joe's father came into the locker room to congratulate him. It was a very special day for Joe. But that wonderful feeling of accomplishment didn't last long.

When Joe reported to practice a couple of days later, he found out that Rick Slager was still the starting quarterback. Joe was upset because he felt that his performance against Northwestern was so strong that he deserved the starting job. Still, Joe didn't give up. Instead, he led the Irish to an incredible comeback victory two weeks later.

When Notre Dame played the University of North Carolina in the fifth game of the season, the Irish were down 14-6 with a little more than five minutes left on the clock. Joe came off the bench to direct two drives that ended in touchdowns, and Notre Dame won 21-14. The next week Joe led an even more dramatic comeback against Air Force. With the Irish trailing 30-10 in the fourth quarter, Joe passed for 134 yards and two touchdowns in the final 13 minutes. The Irish won 31-30!

Joe was playing more, but he still wasn't the starter. "The pattern began to be that Rick Slager would start the game and then Montana would have to come in and save it," former Notre Dame tight end Ken MacAfee remembers.

Notre Dame finished the season with an 8-3 record.

The pattern changed completely the next year. Joe missed all of the 1976 season with a separated shoulder that he suffered during a practice scrimmage. Joe "redshirted" that year, which meant that he still took his scheduled classes but didn't use up one of the three years he was eligible to play varsity football. The word redshirt comes from the color of the jerseys that injured players wore to practice.

During the fall of 1977 Joe came back as the third-string quarterback behind Rusty Lisch and Gary Forystek. (Rick Slager had graduated in 1977.) Both Joe and Coach Devine have their own views about why Joe didn't play much during that stretch. Joe thought that Coach Devine didn't like him and he resented Devine for not playing him more. Coach Devine says that Joe wasn't ready to be the starting quarterback at the beginning of his sophomore season, and that he played Joe in his junior season as soon as Joe received permission from the doctor to play.

The third game of Joe's junior season was the one that turned his career around. The Irish were playing Purdue. Quarterback Rusty Lisch started, but he was replaced in the second half by Gary Forystek. When Gary was injured and knocked out of the game, Devine decided to send Rusty back in the game instead of giving Joe a chance.

"At that moment I felt totally beaten," Joe wrote in *Audibles.* "If I ever thought sincerely about quitting football it was then. That feeling turned to anger and disgust, and I began cursing on the sidelines. I wasn't talking to anyone in particular — I just hoped one of the coaches would hear me. I didn't know if Devine heard me or not and I didn't care."

With just under two minutes to play in the third quarter and the Irish trailing 24-14, Coach Devine was looking for something or someone to turn the game around. He sent in Joe. To give Joe some confidence, Ken MacAfee reminded him of the two comebacks Joe had pulled off during his sophomore season. Joe bobbled the first snap from center and then threw a terrible, inaccurate pass.

In the huddle, Joe used his low-key sense of humor to keep his teammates' spirits up. "That pass was a little off the mark," he said. "The coach is going to really think I'm a jerk." Seconds later, Joe added: "O.K., the butterflies are gone, let's win this thing."

They did, 31-24. He was beginnning to build a reputation for himself as the "Comeback Kid." Not only was Joe able to establish a good mood for the game, he inspired his teammates with his confidence and his leadership. They *knew* he would bring them back when they were behind.

That performance against Purdue won Joe the starting quarterback job for good. For the rest of the season, he continued to show Coach Devine why he deserved it. In a big game at Clemson, Notre Dame found itself trailing by two touchdowns when Joe pulled off a play worthy of a highlight film. When Joe couldn't find an open receiver, he had the choice of running out of bounds or lowering his shoulder and ramming into two Clemson linebackers. Despite the fact that Joe had sat out all of last season with a separated shoulder, he chose to ram into the Clemson linebackers. Coach Devine's heart sank as he thought his top quarterback was going to get hurt. Instead, a stretcher was needed to carry off one of the Clemson linebackers! Joe just trotted back to the huddle.

Coach Devine was impressed. Joe had turned him into a believer. Later that season, Joe impressed his coach off the field. Notre Dame was on the road when Joe knocked on the door of Coach Devine's room at two in the morning. A newspaper article that day quoted Joe in a way that might have made him sound critical of his coach. Joe had tears in his eyes when he said, "Coach, whatever words I used, I never meant it the way it turned out."

"That boy's got class," Coach Devine said later. After a long and difficult stretch, Joe and his coach were no longer at odds with one another.

Notre Dame played its traditional rival, the University of Southern California, later that season. Although USC had beaten the Irish the year before, 17-13, this time the fired-up Notre Dame players burned USC, 49-19. Notre Dame, which had not lost a game since Joe took over as quarterback, was invited to play in the Cotton Bowl, which pits the Southwest Conference winner against any school that is not obligated to play in another bowl through a conference championship.

Joe's Notre Dame team, even with its 10-1 record and Number 2 ranking in the country, was a decided underdog against the University of Texas, which had an 11-0 record and was ranked Number 1 in the 1978 Cotton Bowl. The Texas Longhorns were led by talented running back Earl Campbell, who had won the Heisman Trophy as the best college football player in the country. The Longhorns were also playing in front of their home fans in Dallas, Texas.

The Notre Dame players found inspiration in an unusual source — some Texas players! The week before the game, some of the Longhorns called Notre Dame guard Ernie Hughes and tight end Ken MacAfee "average" blockers. That was all the Fighting Irish needed to hear. They were fighting mad. They also knew that if they beat the team that was ranked first in the country, it was likely that they would be voted the Number 1 team in the country in the polls.

The Notre Dame offensive and defensive lines outblocked the Longhorns and they dominated the line of scrimmage. The Irish won easily, 38-10. After the win over Texas, Notre Dame was ranked Number 1 in the country. A season that had started on the bench for Joe ended with a national championship! The year had been an unbelievable one for Joe, but it was also the one in which his marriage to Kim ended after two years. Joe later said that they were just "too young" when they had married, and it had certainly been a trying two years for Joe at school.

Joe began the next season, which was his last one at Notre Dame, as the team's starting and star quarterback. Joe continued his comeback magic when he threw two touchdown passes and ran for another in the final 14 minutes of a game against Pittsburgh. He turned a 17-7 deficit into a 26-17 Notre Dame victory.

Although Joe's fame increased at Notre Dame, his personality didn't change. He worked hard to be more of an Average Joe than a Super Joe. He still enjoyed playing in Notre Dame's intramural "Bookstore Basketball" championship playoffs, which featured 360 teams, and he continued to shoot pool at Corby's, a bar popular with students.

Joe reached his height of popularity as a college star during the 1979 Cotton Bowl game against the University of Houston. The temperature was just 17 degrees in Dallas that day, and there were 30 mile-per-hour winds. In the fourth quarter, Houston was beating Notre Dame 34-12 while Joe was lying in the locker room with a subnormal body temperature of 96 degrees, instead of the usual 98.6. The team's medical staff covered Joe with blankets and fed him chicken boullion to warm him up. They got his temperature up to normal, and Joe just could not wait any longer. With 7 minutes and 37 seconds left to play, Joe came on to the field. He then completed seven of eight passes for 87 yards and two touchdowns.

With six seconds left on the clock and Notre Dame trailing by six points, Joe had to throw away the ball when his receiver slipped. Now there were two seconds left. Coach Devine was so confident in Joe's ability in the clutch, that he let Joe call the final play. Joe decided to keep the defense off-balance by using the same play he had just tried. This time the receiver, Kris Haines, slipped — into the end zone for a touchdown! Joe Cool had led his team to a dramatic 35-34 victory.

After the Cotton Bowl, Joe was eager to move on to pro football. He would have graduated in the spring of 1978 if he hadn't spent an extra semester at Notre Dame, making up the 1976 football season he missed when he was redshirted. Joe graduated in December and started studying for a career in pro football. Even after all the fireworks in Joe's last two years at Notre Dame, it wasn't going to be easy. When he was being evaluated by the pro teams, one scouting report said: "He's a gutty, gambling, cocky type. Doesn't have great tools but could eventually start."

Once again, Joe was going to have to prove himself.

5

Joe Goes Pro

It may be hard to imagine now, but coaches and scouts in the NFL had doubts that Joe would be successful in the professional ranks. Some teams thought that his arm was not strong enough for the pro game. Others wondered if he was the type of player who couldn't get along with his coach.

NFL teams select players through a college draft, with the team that finished in last place the season before usually getting to pick first from among the college players eligible to enter the pros. Draft choices are very valuable to a team's future and no club wants to waste a high pick on a player who is going to end up sitting on the bench or not making the team. Therefore, scouts judge players very strictly.

"All they care about is how tall a player is, his build, how heavy he is, his delivery, and if he can throw the ball a country mile," explains former 49ers Coach Bill Walsh.

Joe didn't fit neatly into those categories. Although he had grown to be 6'2" and 185 pounds, he was still small by NFL standards. Joe's game did not depend on his throwing the ball a long way. Instead, he relied on accuracy and was able to complete a high percentage of his medium length passes. He did this by moving around in the pocket, protected by linemen who gave him the time to pick out the receiver who was open. This was a style that did not translate easily into great future success in the pros.

But Joe was determined to make it in the pros. He had from December 1978, when he graduated from Notre Dame, until May 1979, when the draft would be held, to prove that he could make it in the big time. He moved to Manhattan Beach, California, outside of Los Angeles. The warm climate would make it easier to work out in the winter. And, like many other top college players who weren't certain first or second round draft choices, he traveled around the country attending workouts conducted by pro football scouts and coaches. Although the people from the NFL can see game films of these players' big college performances, they also want to see the players work out in person.

Joe went to New York to attend a major, combine workout, which allowed him to work out with a number of teams. He also worked out individually for the Green Bay Packers, the Los Angeles Rams, and the San Francisco 49ers. Having moved to sunny Southern California after living in the East and Midwest, Joe discovered that he liked the beaches and warm temperatures. Joe hoped that one of the California teams — the San Francisco 49ers, the Los Angeles Rams, the Los Angeles Raiders (who then played in Northern California as the Oakland Raiders) or the San Diego Chargers — would select him in the NFL draft.

Joe's workout for the 49ers took place in Los Angeles. He threw for 49ers quarterback coach Sam Wyche (now head coach of the Cincinnati Bengals) and head coach Bill Walsh (now a commentator on NBC-TV). For about an hour, Joe threw short "touch" passes to show his control and long "muscle" passes to show his strength.

"The minute I saw him drop back — his quick movement, those quick, nimble feet — I got very serious," Coach Walsh remembers. "I liked everything about Joe. I liked his

41

quickness. I liked his attitude. I particularly liked his willingness to learn. I knew he was a young man who would improve every week. And there was that intangible factor: Joe was a winner all through college. If you're around him any length of time, you can feel it — the confidence. He is a born leader, a champion."

As Coach Walsh left the workout in Los Angeles, he told Joe: "Keep in shape. You might be hearing from us on draft day."

On May 3, 1979, NFL draft day, Joe did indeed hear from the 49ers. They had drafted him in the third round. Joe was the 82nd overall pick. Looking back at Joe's great professional career now, it's hard to believe that there were 81 college players selected ahead of him! Quarterback Phil Simms of Morehead State was selected by the New York Giants and quarterback Steve Fuller of Clemson was selected by the Kansas City Chiefs in the first round.

Joe was thrilled to be going to play for Coach Walsh and the 49ers. He felt that the 49ers were a perfect team for him. The 49ers were a losing team (2-14 the year before) that was in transition. Joe knew that he would have a good chance to play quarterback for the 49ers in the near future.

He had also heard about the great passing game Bill Walsh had developed when he was the coach at Stanford University in 1977-1978. When he was an assistant coach in Cincinnati in the early 1970's, Bill Walsh had helped develop quarterback Ken Anderson. As an assistant coach in San Diego in 1976, Walsh had helped develop Dan Fouts. Both Anderson and Fouts became great NFL quarterbacks. Joe would definitely be learning his trade from one of the best.

Once Joe was drafted by San Francisco, Joe's agent, Larry Muno, and the 49ers had to agree upon a contract. Joe and his agent put up a tough fight and ended up getting a three-year contract that gave Joc a $50,000 signing bonus and a base salary of $50,000, $70,000, and $85,000 for the three years. That was a lot of money to Joe at the time, although it seems like very little compared to the multi-million dollar contracts he signed later in his career.

At the 49ers' training camp in 1979, Joe wasn't thinking about money. He was concentrating on making the team. When Joe first arrived at camp, people couldn't believe how thin he was.

"I was sitting next to him at the counter in Howard Johnson's," says former 49ers wide receiver Dwight Clark, a 10th-round draft pick that same year who became Joe's good friend and one of his favorite receivers. "Long blond hair, Fu Manchu mustache, skinny legs. I thought, 'This guy must be a kicker.' Then he introduced himself, and I couldn't believe this was the guy who brought Notre Dame back to beat us in the fourth quarter when I was at Clemson."

Joe and Dwight were roommates at training camp. They were both homesick and they were both afraid of being cut from the team. They would sneak in the back door at breakfast because a man named Max McCartney sat in the front. Max was known to players as Max the Axe because it was his job to tell the players, "Coach wants to see you." This meant that they were being cut (or axed) from the team. Max the Axe never got to Joe or Dwight.

Coach Walsh was grooming Joe to be the 49ers quarterback of the future and was bringing him along slowly. Quarterbacks need time to make a successful transition from college football to pro football. Quarterbacks have to learn lots of new plays and must deal with much more sophisticated defenses. They also must learn how to deal with the pressure on and off the field. This process can take as long as three or four years, which is longer than it takes most top college running backs and receivers to adjust to the pro game.

Joe spent a lot of his rookie season memorizing the numbers and words used by the quarterback when he shouts out plays. The 49ers' numbering system was very different from the one Joe used at Notre Dame. Joe had to prove to the 49ers coaches that he knew the plays. Otherwise, they wouldn't even let him into a game. Joe also had to learn his receivers' moves and habits so that he could anticipate where they would run on the field.

Steve DeBerg was the starting quarterback for that season. He had once broken an NFL record for completions. Joe started one game, played a little in two other games, and made brief appearances in the other 13 games. "My first [exhibition game] start my rookie year I threw two touchdowns — to the other team," Joe said. "On one of those interceptions, the guy ran me over at the one-yard line."

To build Joe's confidence, Coach Walsh would put Joe in the game at the end of a 49ers drive. Steve DeBerg would march the 49ers down to the opponent's five-yard line, and then Joe would come off the bench and lead the team to a touchdown. It was not a bad way to spend his first season in the pros, although the 49ers did not score all that often — they were 2-14 for the second straight year.

During that rookie season, Joe was also busy off the field. He got married for the second time. His wife, Cass, was a flight attendant whom Joe met during a flight to Los Angeles at the end of his senior season at Notre Dame. The financial security Joe's contract provided allowed for a change in his lifestyle. He could afford things he couldn't have dreamed of before. He and Cass bought a house in Skyline, California, and Cass quit her job so she wouldn't have to travel all the time. They also bought two Arabian horses, Simmy and Mac, and enjoyed riding them through the hills near their home, although Joe did not ride during the season because of the risk of injury.

In his second season with the 49ers, Joe started 7 of the team's last 10 games and led the NFL with a .654 completion percentage. That was when Coach Walsh decided Joe was going to be his number 1 quarterback, although he didn't let anyone know right away. Joe was learning Coach Walsh's short and safe passing game, which was perfectly suited to Joe's style of play.

It was during this season that Joe and Dwight Clark began to form a dynamic passing duo. They spent long hours after practice working together on pass patterns and they came to know instinctively what each would do on the field.

"Everyone said there was a chemistry between us," Dwight Clark told *Sports Illustrated*. "Joe once said in an interview, 'I can look all around the field. I can look away and still come back and find Dwight, that big, slow, loping receiver.' He could see me moving across the field."

The 49ers won 6 and lost 10 during the 1980 season, but the team had improved tremendously over the previous season. The offensive line had now played together for a few years and was ready for greatness. The 49ers defensive backfield was very aggressive in defending against the pass and was rapidly gaining respect from opposing teams. The 1980 49ers were a team on the rise.

Then came Joe's big break. Steve DeBerg was traded to the Denver Broncos before the 1981 season. Joe had won the job as starting quarterback for the 49ers!

6

Joe's First Super Bowl

As the 49ers' plane flew over the city of Pittsburgh on its way to the airport, Joe Montana leaned over to look out the window. Below, he could see Three Rivers Stadium, the home of the Pittsburgh Steelers. Joe and the 49ers were playing the Steelers in Game 9 of the 1981 NFL season.

Joe's mind was filled with memories. He had rooted for the Steelers when he was a boy growing up in Monongahela. The Steelers had won the Super Bowl in 1979 and 1980. It would be the first time Joe would see the Steelers play live.

Joe and his teammates didn't play particularly well in Pittsburgh, but they played well enough to win, 17-14. For the 49ers, who had started the season by losing two of their first three games, it was their sixth straight win. That was quite a turnaround from their 6-10 record the year before. The 49ers were the surprise of the league and they were receiving a great deal of national publicity. Joe was also getting a lot of recognition since this was only his first full season as a starter.

Joe had worked hard for that recognition. The job of a starting quarterback in the NFL consists of a lot more than just putting on a helmet for three hours on Sunday afternoon. Joe often spent at least two hours a day studying plays between practice sessions. Then he would head home with two or three reels of game films to watch.

Under Coach Bill Walsh, the 49ers usually went into games with 75 to 80 set passing plays, and some of them had many variations. One time, Joe went into a game having to remember more than 100 pass plays. Add 35 running plays and that means Joe went into many games having to remember between 100 and 135 plays.

During a game Coach Walsh and his assistant coaches would call the plays by sending them in with a substitute player while the team was in the huddle. But Coach Walsh also expected his quarterback to be creative enough to call an audible and change the play at the line of scrimmage, if the quarterback didn't think a specific play would work against the defense the opposing team had put in. When a quarterback calls an audible, he uses a secret code of numbers or words to tell his teammates the new play.

Coach Walsh tried to make Joe's job on the field a little easier by introducing what he called his script system. That meant that the first 25 offensive plays that the 49ers would run in a game were given to Joe by Coach Walsh before the game started. This way, Joe and his teammates didn't have to worry about what plays were going to be called early in a game and they had time to get adjusted to the flow of the action. If the 49ers were faced with an unusual situation (such as first and goal at the opponent's five-yard line), the script was not followed and appropriate plays for that situation were called.

Joe worked hard on Coach Walsh's system with 49ers assistant coach Sam Wyche, and assistant Paul Hackett. Coach Walsh's offensive system was different from those used by most other teams in the NFL back in 1981.

Today, teams pass the ball all the time. But back then it was traditional for teams to run the football for short yardage on first and second downs, and then throw only when they needed five yards or more on third down. Coach Walsh would pass when other teams would run. The run was used mostly to make the defense worry about both the pass and the run. Many times, the quarterback would fake a handoff to one of the running backs before stepping back to pass. This was called a play-action pass. It forces the linebackers to come in and protect against the run. When the linebackers come in, the receivers are open for the pass.

To make Coach Walsh's offense work, the quarterback needed a lot of choices, or options, when it came to which receiver he would pass to. An opposing defense might be able to contain the primary receiver or even stop the 49ers' first two options on a play, but the 49ers would always have a good third or fourth option.

Joe was the ideal quarterback for Coach Walsh's play-action system because he is so skillful at avoiding a pass rush by scrambling and then throwing off-balance while on the run. The 49ers actually practiced the scrambling throw because it was such a key part of their offense.

"Our scramble drills cover all the possibilities," Russ Francis, a former 49ers tight end, once told a reporter. "It's a relief to run down the field and see nothing but trouble, everything getting very hairy, and as you turn your head you see Joe Montana scrambling. He has seen the problem before you get there and now he's going to finish the play anyway. And you know he *will* finish it."

Joe's 49ers teammates were gaining the same type of confidence in him that his Notre Dame teammates had. They felt that when Joe was on the field, something good was going to happen. As he grew more familiar with Coach Walsh's system, Joe was able to use his own talents to make the 49ers offense run even better. Besides his scrambling ability and his good judgment in calling audibles, Joe and his receivers — Dwight Clark and Freddie Solomon — were beginning to know each other's moves so well they seemed to be able to read each other's minds. Even if a play broke down, a receiver would run right to an open spot on the field just as Joe threw the ball there — without either one of them waving or saying a word.

The San Francisco 49ers fans were equally impressed with Joe. When *The San Francisco Chronicle* held a contest to select a nickname for Joe, readers suggested more than 10,000 names. There was Joe Cool, Frisco Kid, Gold

Flinger, Cable Car Joe, and Sir Pass. About 200 fans jokingly suggested Beaut, a play on words referring to the city of Butte, Montana. When Joe was asked to select the winner from among the 12 finalists, he chose Big Sky, which is the nickname of the state of Montana but also says a lot about how Joe was throwing the football. During the 1981 season, Joe completed 64 percent of his passes, threw for 3,565 yards and 19 touchdowns, and finished the season as the highest-ranked quarterback in the conference.

The 49ers had two long winning streaks that season. After beating the Steelers and the Atlanta Falcons to run their victory streak to seven games, the 49ers lost to the Cleveland Browns 15-12. They then won their next five straight to finish the regular season at 13-3, which was the best record in the league. The 49ers became the first team since the Chicago Bears of 1945-46-47 to go from the league's worst record (the 49ers were 2-14 in 1979) to the league's best in just three years.

The 49ers had won the NFC Western Division title and were in the playoffs for the first time in eight years. Their first opponent, in the semifinal game, was the New York Giants, a team they had beaten 17-10 during the regular season. Playing at home in Candlestick Park, the 49ers defeated the Giants, 38-24, to advance to the NFC Championship game. The 49ers were going to face the Dallas Cowboys, known at the time as America's Team because they had so many fans all over the country.

Although the 49ers had beaten the Cowboys 45-14, earlier in the season, they knew they could not take Dallas lightly. The Cowboys had been caught by surprise against the upstart 49ers in that first game, and Dallas now was playing well enough to have whipped the Tampa Bay Buccaneers 38-0 in the other NFC semifinal game. Their famous Doomsday Defense was definitely something for opposing quarterbacks to fear.

The NFC Championship game between Dallas and San Francisco turned out to be a classic. The 49ers jumped out to a 7-0 lead when Joe ducked under charging Cowboys lineman Ed "Too Tall" Jones and hit Dwight Clark with a 30-yard pass. But the Cowboys came back with a field goal and a touchdown to take a 10-7 advantage. Joe threw another touchdown pass to Dwight Clark, this one for 26 yards, and the 49ers were up 14-10. The Cowboys came back to score a touchdown on a run by running back Tony Dorsett at the end of the second quarter and Dallas was on top at halftime, 17-14.

The game continued to seesaw in the second half as the tension increased with the conference championship on the line. The 49ers scored another touchdown to take the lead, but the Cowboys came back after a 49ers' fumble to score a touchdown of their own, giving them a 27-21 lead with only 4:19 left in the game.

If Joe was going to live up to the nickname of the Comeback Kid in the pros, this was the time to do it. The 49ers offense took over all the way back on their own 11-yard line. With the Cowboys playing for the pass, Coach Walsh mixed in some running plays with his passing plays and Joe was able to move the team all the way down to the Cowboys six-yard line.

But then Joe began having trouble. On second down, he missed Freddie Solomon with a pass that would have scored the winning touchdown. There were only 58 seconds left in the game. Joe gulped. He was worrying about choking under pressure and losing the game.

Now, it was third down. Joe dropped back to pass and was quickly pressured by three Cowboys defenders. He raced to his right and saw Dwight Clark cutting across the back of the end zone. Joe faked a throw on the rushing linemen to get them to stop running and jump in the air. It worked. Joe had just enough time to throw the ball deep into the end zone. Dwight leaped with his arms stretched out over his head and caught the ball for the winning touchdown. This became known as The Catch. The victory meant the San Francisco 49ers were going to face the Cincinnati Bengals in the 1982 Super Bowl!

Super Bowl XVI was played at the Pontiac Silverdome in Pontiac, Michigan, which was the same stadium where the 49ers had lost their opening game of the season against the Detroit Lions. They'd come a long way since then.

On the day of the big game, the temperature, with the wind chill factor, felt like 30 degrees below zero. The players were thankful the game was being played indoors. Since they wouldn't have the cold to deal with, they could concentrate on their plays. The 49ers had come prepared with enough new plays to fill a playbook. One of them was the Triple Pass, in which Joe handed off to running back Ricky Patton, who handed the ball to Freddie Solomon, who pitched back to Joe, who threw downfield to tight end Charle

Young. Another was the End-Around Pass, with Dwight Clark throwing the ball to Freddie Solomon.

Using their dazzling offensive game plan, the 49ers caught the Bengals flat-footed and raced out to a 20-0 lead in the first half. Cincinnati came back to make the score close, but the 49ers defense rose to the challenge and stopped the Bengals short of the goal line late in the fourth quarter. The 49ers won the Super Bowl 26-21! Joe completed 14 of 22 passes for 157 yards and was named the Most Valuable Player of the game. With his Super Bowl victory, Joe Montana joined Joe Namath as the only quarterbacks who had won both a national championship in college and a Super Bowl in the pros.

The morning following Super Bowl XVI, Joe woke up very early to appear on the morning shows of the three major television networks — NBC's *Today*, ABC's *Good Morning America*, and CBS' *This Morning*. At a luncheon that afternoon, Joe accepted a new red Firebird Trans Am for being named the Most Valuable Player.

There were plenty of awards to go around for the rest of the 49ers, too. Coach Walsh was named Coach of the Year in the NFL, and six 49ers were named to start in the Pro-

Bowl, which is the NFL all-star game.

Soon after the Super Bowl, while Joe was home in Monongahela to see his folks, the Montanas were visited by a Canadian film crew that was making a documentary on Joe, basketball player Larry Bird, hockey player Wayne Gretzky and baseball player Gary Carter. The director asked Joe and his dad to return to the Polonolises' backyard so they could film Joe throwing passes to his dad, just as he had done years before.

At the director's suggestion, Joe threw one pass far enough in front so that his dad would have to dive for the ball. Sure enough, Mr. Montana left his feet to catch the ball. He hit the ground hard and tumbled in the grass, but he came up laughing.

Joe might be a Super Bowl hero, but when it came to his relationship with his dad, nothing had changed between them.

7

Riding the Roller Coaster

As the hero of the 1982 Super Bowl, Joe was now a celebrity. Everyone wanted some of his time. The press wanted interviews. Fans wanted autographs. Businesses wanted Joe to speak at their conventions and shake hands with their customers. Companies wanted him to appear in newspaper and magazine advertisements and on television commercials to endorse their products. They would pay Joe to tell the audience that he, Joe Montana, used their product and thought it was terrific. As they say in the advertising business, Joe was hot.

And he was rich. After the Super Bowl, the 49ers rewarded their star quarterback with a four-year contract worth more than $1.5 million, an average of $375,000 a year. That was a huge pile of money for a pro football player to be making at the time. Joe was getting a taste of the good life in professional football. But he would soon find out that success can sometimes lead to a whole new assortment of problems.

In that summer of 1982, when the 49ers players and coaches gathered to begin pre-season practice, they knew that it would be difficult to defend their title. Champions have to contend with hungry opponents every week. To the other teams, beating the champ is a very big deal, and each week's game becomes like a mini-Super Bowl for them.

It is also hard to maintain the same unselfish winning chemistry on a team the year after it has won a championship. Members of the team become jealous of the attention others get from reporters. Some players get big heads after winning and they forget how hard they had to work to get to the top of their game. They do not have the same drive or desire that they had the season before.

Players also get a year older and possibly a step slower. Others get traded. New players join the team, which sometimes changes the relationships among returning players.

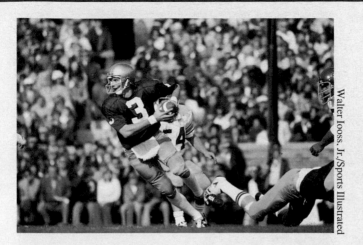

Even in college, Joe was famous for making big plays in the clutch and directing his team to come-from-behind victories. As a Notre Dame senior playing against Houston in the 1979 Cotton Bowl, Joe was facing a 34-12 deficit with 7:37 to play. Even though he was sick most of the game, he led his team to a 35-34 win.

The Last Ten Super Bowl MVPs

XXV	-	Otis Anderson, New York Giants (HB)
XXIV	-	**Joe Montana, San Francisco (QB)**
XXIII	-	**Jerry Rice, San Francisco (WR)**
XXII	-	Doug Williams, Washington (QB)
XXI	-	Phil Simms, New York Giants (QB)
XX	-	Richard Dent, Chicago (DE)
XIX	-	**Joe Montana, San Francisco (QB)**
XVIII	-	Marcus Allen, Los Angeles Raiders (RB)
XVII	-	John Riggins, Washington (RB)
XVI	-	**Joe Montana, San Francisco (QB)**

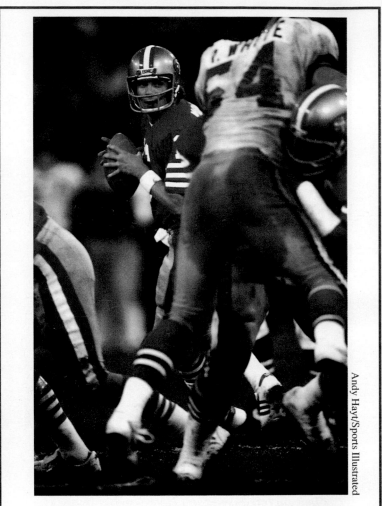

Andy Hayt/Sports Illustrated

After dodging these defenders, Joe was able to connect with receiver Dwight Clark in the 1982 NFC title game against the Dallas Cowboys. What came to be called "The Catch" gave the 49ers the win, 28-27.

Heinz Kluetmeier/Sports Illustrated

Fighting off a fourth-quarter comeback by the Cincinnati Bengals in Super Bowl XVI in 1982, Joe made key passes to keep the 49ers on top. San Francisco won the game, 26-21, and Joe garnered his first MVP honors. He passed for 157 yards and 1 touchdown. Number 16 also ran for 18 yards and a touchdown.

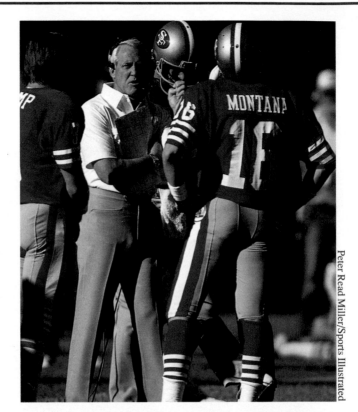

Joe and former 49ers head coach Bill Walsh worked well together. Joe's accurate passing, mobility, and ability to think on his feet made him the perfect quarterback to run Coach Walsh's passing offense. Under Coach Walsh, the 49ers had a record of 102-64 from 1979 through 1988, and won three Super Bowls. George Siefert took over the 49ers in 1989 and coached the team to another Super Bowl victory.

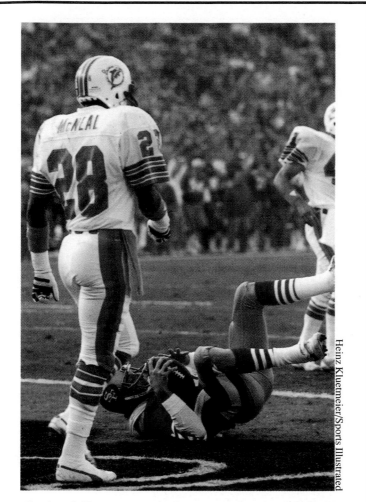

Heinz Kluetmeier/Sports Illustrated

Joe's ability to run and pass makes him doubly dangerous to opposing defenses. In the 49ers' 38-16 win over the Miami Dolphins in Super Bowl XIX in 1985, Joe ran for 59 yards — and this touchdown — and passed for 331 yards, too!

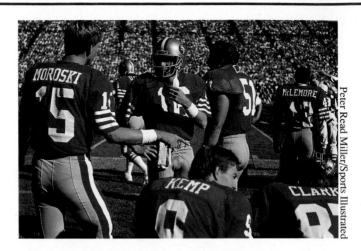

Returning with a bang only 55 days after back surgery, Joe completed 13 of 19 passes for 270 yards and 3 touchdowns on November 9, 1986, in a game against the St. Louis Cardinals. The 49ers walloped the Cardinals 43-17.

Joe Versus the All-Time Greats

Player	Career	Comp.%	TD	Yards
Joe Montana	**1979-1990**	**63.7**	**242**	**34,910**
Dan Marino	1983-1990	59.3	240	31,224
Bart Starr	1956-1971	57.4	152	24,718
Sonny Jurgensen	1957-1974	57.1	255	32,224
Roger Staubach	1969-1979	57.0	153	22,700
Fran Tarkenton	1961-1978	57.0	342	47,003
Sammy Baugh	1937-1952	56.5	187	21,886
Bob Griese	1967-1980	56.2	192	25,092
Otto Graham	1950-1955	55.7	88	13,499
Y.A. Tittle	1950-1964	55.5	212	28,339
John Unitas	1956-1973	54.6	290	40,239
Norm Van Brocklin	1949-1960	53.6	173	23,611

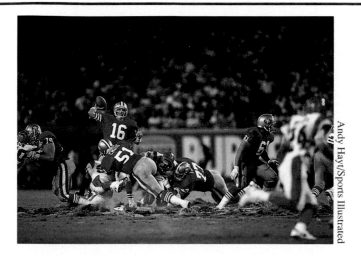

In the 1989 Super Bowl, the 49ers were losing to the Cincinnati Bengals 16-13. With just 3:10 left to play, Joe marched the 49ers 92 yards in 11 plays — touchdown! The 49ers won 20-16.

1990's Top Ten Quarterbacks

Player	NFL Rating Points*
Jim Kelly, Bills	101.2
Warren Moon, Oilers	96.6
Steve DeBerg, Chiefs	96.3
Phil Simms, Giants	92.7
Randall Cunningham, Eagles	91.6
Jay Schroeder, Raiders	90.6
Joe Montana, 49ers	**89.0**
Dan Marino, Dolphins	82.6
Jim Harbaugh, Bears	81.9
Bubby Brister, Steelers	81.6

* The league's measure of overall passing efficiency.

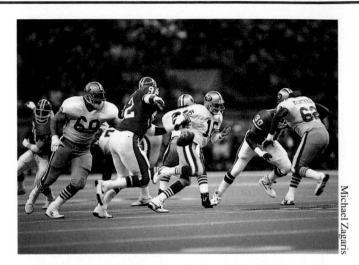

Demonstrating his running ability, Joe scrambled for 10 yards in Super Bowl XXIV against the Denver Broncos in January 1990. The 49ers ran all over the Broncos, clobbering them 55-10, and Joe was named the Most Valuable Player. He was unstoppable in the 1990 regular season, throwing for 3,944 yards and 26 touchdowns.

1990 San Francisco Rushing Leaders

	Yards	Touchdowns
Dexter Carter	460	1
Roger Craig	439	1
Tom Rathman	315	7
Harry Sydney	166	3
Joe Montana	162	1

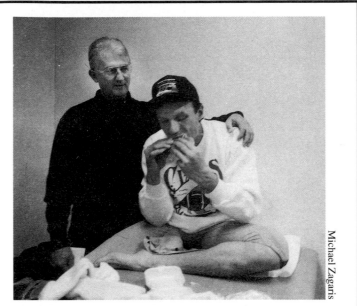

Michael Zagaris

Winning the Super Bowl can make anyone hungry. After the 49ers beat the Broncos in the 1990 Super Bowl, Joe shared a hamburger with his dad in the locker room.

Teams with the Best Super Bowl Records

	Appearances	W	L
San Francisco 49ers	4	4	0
Pittsburgh Steelers	4	4	0
Oakland/L.A. Raiders	4	3	1
Washington Redskins	4	2	2
Dallas Cowboys	5	2	3
Miami Dolphins	5	2	3

Balloons and music filled the air as Joe celebrated with his wife, Jennifer, and his daughters, Alexandra and Elizabeth, in a parade through the crowded streets of San Francisco saluting the 49ers' win over the Denver Broncos in Super Bowl XXIV.

Last Ten Super Bowl Champs

1991	-	XXV	-	New York Giants
1990	-	XXIV	-	**San Francisco 49ers**
1989	-	XXIII	-	**San Francisco 49ers**
1988	-	XXII	-	Washington Redskins
1987	-	XXI	-	New York Giants
1986	-	XX	-	Chicago Bears
1985	-	XIX	-	**San Francisco 49ers**
1984	-	XVIII	-	Los Angeles Raiders
1983	-	XVII	-	Washington Redskins
1982	-	XVI	-	**San Francisco 49ers**

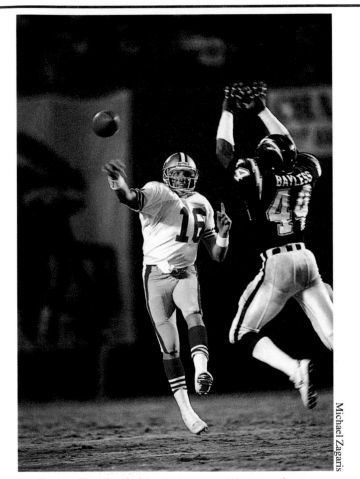

Michael Zagaris

Joe unleashed this pass as a Charger leapt in his face during a 1990 exhibition game. The San Diego Chargers narrowly beat San Francisco 22-21. However, the Rams and the Saints were the only teams who could beat the 49ers during the regular season.

Michael Zagaris

At halftime of every game, Joe meets with 49ers offensive coordinator Mike Holmgren to plan their strategy for the second half. The quarterback and coach can compare what Joe has seen on the field with what Coach Holmgren has seen from his bird's-eye view in the pressbox.

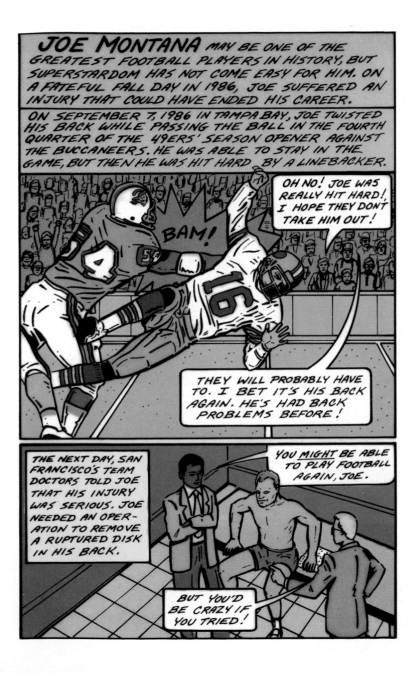

JOE WAS RELEASED FROM THE HOSPITAL EXACTLY ONE WEEK AFTER HIS OPERATION. SAN FRANCISCO COACH BILL WALSH DID NOT EXPECT JOE BACK THAT SEASON. HOWEVER, JOE WORKED HARD TO GET BACK IN SHAPE, AND THE DOCTORS TOLD HIM HE MIGHT BE ABLE TO PLAY BY DECEMBER.

DO YOU THINK JOE WILL BE ABLE TO COME BACK THIS SEASON?

NO WAY! IF HE TAKES ONE HIT, HIS BACK WILL CRUMBLE!

INCREDIBLY, JOE WAS BACK ON THE FIELD PRACTICING WITH THE TEAM AND STRENGTHENING HIS MUSCLES ONLY ONE MONTH AFTER THE OPERATION. THE TOUGHEST EXERCISE FOR HIM WAS THE SOCK DRILL, DESIGNED TO HELP JOE'S LEGS AND BACK. A LEAD-FILLED SOCK WOULD BE TOSSED 5 TO 15 YARDS TO HIS LEFT OR RIGHT, OVER AND OVER. JOE WOULD HAVE TO TWIST AND SPIN, RACING OVER TO WHERE THE SOCK HAD DROPPED. HE WOULD THEN SET UP TO PASS. IMMEDIATELY, ANOTHER SOCK WAS TOSSED AND HE WOULD REPEAT THE DRILL.

I KNOW IT HURTS, JOE, BUT YOU HAVE TO DO THIS IF YOU WANT TO PLAY AGAIN.

The media — newspaper, radio, and TV reporters — place every move the team makes under a microscope, putting even more pressure on the players and coaches. And there is always the unpredictable factor of injuries to key players.

All of these things would happen to the 49ers. And on top of it all, 1982 was also the first season in which the NFL players went on strike. The strike would interrupt the season, cause the cancellation of seven games, and disrupt the team unity of the 49ers players, many of whom disagreed about whether or not they should be out on strike.

The friction began during training camp in the summer, when talk first started about a possible strike. At that time, Joe and teammate Ray Wersching, the 49ers kicker, announced their resignations from the players' union, which was called the National Football League Players Association (NFLPA). Joe said he did not believe in what the union was fighting for and he did not have much confidence in Ed Garvey, who was the executive director of the NFLPA.

The union wanted a share of the money the owners made from sales of tickets, food, and souvenirs to the fans and also part of the money the television networks paid the owners for the rights to televise NFL games. Joe believed the players should have been fighting instead for a system of free agency like the one that major league baseball players had. In baseball, players were not bound to their teams like football players were when their contracts ran out. Baseball players had the right to sign with the team that offered them the best deal. Joe thought this would be a better way of increasing salaries in pro football.

The NFLPA called for the players to go on strike two games into the season. But by that time the 49ers' own season was already in trouble. Plagued with injuries, the team had lost its first two games. Bickering had already begun among the players and the coaches, who were blaming each other for the team's problems.

The players had very strong feelings about the issues of the strike. Most were in favor of the strike, but several were opposed to it, and this pulled the team apart. Some of his teammates said that Joe didn't want to strike because he was making a lot of money and he didn't want to lose any of it. But Joe felt that he was fighting for something that *all* the players wanted. It was a very emotional argument and neither side could see the other's point of view.

During the first few weeks of what turned out to be an

eight-week strike, Joe and his teammates practiced together as often as five days a week. But as the strike continued, the number of practices decreased. When he wasn't practicing and exercising to stay in shape, Joe did some sports interviews and features for the local ABC television affiliate in San Francisco.

The NFL season resumed after a 57-day strike. Joe ended up losing $140,000 in salary. None of the players benefited from the strike. The experience only served to hurt the morale of many teams.

In the 49ers' first game after the strike, Joe completed 26 of 39 passes for 408 yards and three touchdowns in a 31-20 win over the St. Louis Cardinals, but it was downhill for the 49ers after that. Some members of the team weren't talking to one another because of the strike. The 49ers definitely weren't playing as a unit. They finished the strike-shortened season with a 3-6 record and they did not qualify for the playoffs.

For Joe, the hard times continued. Joe and his wife Cass were not getting along, and during the following season, they would get divorced. Cass wanted Joe to be at home more and that just didn't fit in with the life of a professional football player. It would be the second time Joe's marriage had ended in divorce.

Joe's relationship with Coach Walsh also was not going smoothly. The 1983 season was Joe's third season as the 49ers regular starting quarterback. A lot had been written in newspapers and magazines about Coach Walsh's brilliant offensive system and about how perfectly suited Joe was to run it. As is often the case between two stars who have very strong egos, such as Coach Walsh and Joe Montana, each believed at the time that he was more responsible for the team's success. Joe felt that he wasn't being given the credit he deserved for the 49ers' success.

"Let's face it, the underlying basis of any friction between Bill and me is his desire for people to believe I am one of the better quarterbacks in the game because of his offensive system," Joe wrote in his autobiography, *Audibles*. "My feeling is that Bill's system and the quarterback work hand in hand. I believe you need the right person to play within the system. Not any quarterback could achieve what I have simply because of a coach's system."

Coach Walsh had been critical of Joe because he felt that Joe was devoting too much time to off-the-field activities in the season after the 49ers won the Super Bowl. Joe claimed that since he shot commercials and made appearances on his own time, he wasn't doing anything to hurt the team. It was not as though he was out of shape or he was missing practices or games.

Over the years, Joe has said that he learned a lot about football and some things about life from Coach Walsh. The two men soon realized that they would have to make room for each other's egos in order for the team to be successful.

In the 1983 season, the 49ers were back to their old form on the field. Without the strike and the bad luck of injuries, they showed they were still a talented team. The 49ers went 10-6 during the regular season to qualify for the playoffs.

In the 1983 playoffs, the 49ers edged the Detroit Lions, 24-23, to advance to the NFC championship game. In a game against the Washington Redskins played at Robert F. Kennedy Memorial Stadium in Washington, D.C., Joe brought the 49ers back from a 21-0 deficit late in the third quarter. But the Redskins won 24-21 on Mark Moseley's 25-yard field goal with just 40 seconds left in the game.

Joe said the playoff loss to the Redskins was one of the

toughest he ever experienced. "That particular day I vowed we would make it to the next Super Bowl," Joe wrote in his autobiography. "Not only would we make it, we would win it."

How right Joe would turn out to be. But a lot happened to Joe between the loss to Washington and the start of training camp the next season.

Joe met Jennifer Wallace, who was a model and a television actress, when Joe was in Los Angeles to shoot a commercial for Schick razors. In the commercial, the Schick Sheriff (played by Jennifer) gets the cowboy (played by Joe) to buy her brand of razor.

The two soon began dating, and during that off-season, Joe would visit Jennifer in Southern California, where she lived. They also began exercising together. In the past, Joe had played tennis and golf during the off-season to stay in shape for football. Jennifer convinced Joe to join her for aerobics classes and to run with her, something Joe had never done before. Sometimes, she'd even needle him to run 50 yards straight up a sand dune. It was harder than Joe had ever exercised, and he complained a lot. But the hard work paid off. "I never felt better coming to camp," he said.

Before the season started, Joe felt ready to ask Jennifer to marry him. But he wasn't sure how he was going to propose. Finally, Joe decided to hire a plane that would fly by with a streamer that read: JEN, WILL YOU MARRY ME? JOE.

Joe took Jennifer to their favorite park in San Francisco, the Marina Green. He had arranged for the pilot to fly by with the streamer while they were there. Joe kept walking around the park with Jennifer, but where was the plane? Jennifer wanted to know what was going on. Finally, the plane flew overhead.

"I looked up, and the streamer was backwards," Joe remembers. "I said, 'Oh God.' We were on the wrong side of it. I started maneuvering her around. She said, 'Joe, what are you doing?' Finally she saw it. She said, 'Yes,' right away. I was ready for her to say, 'No.' Then she said, 'What took you so long?'"

Joe and Jennifer became engaged and planned to get married after the season, which they hoped would end with a second visit to the Super Bowl. Joe, now 28, was ready to settle down and raise a family. He certainly could afford one. After his strong 1983 season, the 49ers rewarded Joe with a new contract that made him a millionaire; the 49ers would pay him $6.3 million over six years.

Joe was ready to make good on his vow to return to the Super Bowl. He proceeded to lead the 49ers to a memorable 1984 season. They went 15-1 to become the first NFL team to win 15 games during the regular season. In the playoffs, they beat the New York Giants, 21-10, and then ousted the Chicago Bears, 23-0, to reach the Super Bowl. Joe received his highest NFL quarterback rating (102.9). The rating, which measures a quarterback's passing efficiency, is based on his percentage of touchdown passes per passing attempt, percentage of completions per attempt, percentage of interceptions per attempt, and average yards gained per attempt.

But even with such high marks, Joe was miffed that he was not getting the kind of recognition he wanted from the media and the fans as the top quarterback in the game. Everyone was talking about this new kid, Dan Marino of the Miami Dolphins, who would be the 49ers' opponents in the Super Bowl.

The 1985 Super Bowl against Miami was like a home game for the 49ers because it was played at Stanford Stadium in Palo Alto, California, which is outside San Francisco.

During the pre-Super Bowl hype, all the talk was about Dan Marino, who had thrown an incredible 48 touchdown passes during the regular season and another 7 touchdown passes in two playoff games. The media wasn't concerned with what Joe Montana might do — they wanted to know how the 49ers would try to contain Marino.

Joe was upset, but he kept his cool. He knew he had something to prove, and he did just that. Playing behind an offensive line that gave him great protection, Joe completed 24 of 35 passes for 331 yards and three touchdowns and no interceptions. He showed everyone who the fastest gun in the West was when he hit halfback Carl Monroe on a 33-yard TD pass over the middle in the first quarter. He scrambled for 6 yards to score one touchdown and for another 12 to set up a field goal. He scrambled away from the Miami pass rush to throw a 40-yard strike to running back Wendell Tyler to set up another touchdown. When the smoke had cleared, the final score was San Francisco 38, Miami 16.

Joe felt that his second Super Bowl victory was extra special because many of his teammates were the same guys who had been part of the first Super Bowl team. They were also the guys who had gone through a tough time during the

1982 players' strike. The players and coaches had made a tremendous effort to put their differences behind them and regain the close feeling that had existed before the strike, when they won their first Super Bowl.

"For me, it's been like growing up with a family," Joe said. "Relating to the same people day after day, year after year, is special. The fellows on the 49ers are special. They're the brothers I never had."

The 49er family added one more member in February when Joe and Jennifer were married.

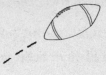

8

A Very Difficult Season

The more the 49ers won and the bigger a celebrity Joe became, the harder it was for him to go out anywhere in San Francisco without being hounded for autographs. Joe didn't blame the fans; he appreciated their support and was happy to meet them. But even a star quarterback needs to be able to go grocery shopping, to go to the movies, or just to go out with his wife for a quiet dinner without having to sign autographs the whole time. The crowds had gotten so big outside the 49ers locker room after games that Joe needed to have a private security guard walk him to the team bus. Sometimes, the guard had to sneak Joe out of the stadium, through side doors or behind the food counters.

This was a different kind of popularity than Joe had been used to. He had always been generous with his time when it came to working with charitable organizations, especially when kids were involved. Once, Joe was contacted by a representative of the Sacramento branch of the Make-A-Wish Foundation, an organization that tries to grant the wishes of very ill children. The person was calling about 11-year-old Matthew Hart. Matthew had a brain tumor and was at the University of California at San Francisco Hospital. The doctors told Matthew's parents that he had 48 hours to live. The Make-A-Wish Foundation people learned that Matthew's favorite player was Joe Montana.

Joe was on his way to sign a new contract extension when a team representative called Joe at home and told him about Matthew. Joe changed his route and stopped by the hospital. "He was beautiful," remembers Ronie Saake of the Sacramento Make-A-Wish Foundation. "He wasn't some guy who was saying, 'I'm a superstar here to help.' He said he was honored and humbled that Matt had asked for him."

Joe met with Matt for 45 minutes. Matt went in and out of consciousness, but he would grab Joe's hand every time he woke up just to make sure that he was really with Joe

Montana. Three weeks later, Matt was able to walk out of the hospital. Matt was still sick the following September, but he was able to go to a 49ers game as Joe's guest.

During lunch breaks at training camp, Joe almost always signs autographs at the 49ers offices. Often there are cartons upon cartons filled with letters to Joe. The letters come from as far away as France, Ireland, and Japan.

Joe doesn't mind being famous, but what makes him happiest is being at home with his wife and his kids. Joe's first child, a daughter named Alexandra, was born on October 2, 1985, during the season right after the 49ers won their second Super Bowl.

It was during that 1985 season, just before and after Alexandra was born, that Joe learned how difficult life can sometimes be when you're a famous football player.

Joe's 1985 season began poorly and went downhill from there. During training camp, he started feeling severe lower-back pain. Because of the pain, Joe wasn't able to loosen up the way he usually did, but he still didn't pay a lot of attention to it. Like most NFL quarterbacks, he had learned to live with a few aches and pains.

But then Joe's pain got worse. To help relax his back,

he spent a lot of time working out in a swimming pool in Rocklin, California, which is where the 49ers summer training camp is held. He wore a jacket around his waist so that he would keep afloat while walking back and forth in the pool. Joe missed a couple of exhibition games, but he was in the lineup for the 49ers' regular season opener against the Minnesota Vikings.

The 49ers lost that first game to the Vikings, 28-21. It was the first of six frustrating losses the team would suffer that season. The 49ers lost five of those games by a total of 20 points, for an average of 4 points a game.

Early in the season, with the team struggling, Joe was even booed by the hometown crowd in San Francisco. The crowd's reaction annoyed Joe, as did the many nasty letters he received from fans during that stretch. One fan said he'd left one 49ers game early because the team looked so bad. He described the 49ers' play as "Mickey Mouse."

Joe had had it. He wrote back on 49ers stationery: "I'm glad you left the game early. We don't need your kind of support. You're not a real 49er faithful. Hope you enjoy watching TV." After his signature, Joe added: "P.S. Suggest you subscribe to the Disney Channel if you like Mickey

Mouse." The letter became public when the fan sent it to *San Francisco Chronicle* columnist Glenn Dickey. It seemed to be out of character for Joe to get mad like that, and Joe agreed. But he explained that he felt the fans expected too much of the 49ers after they had won 18 games and lost only 1 on their way to winning the Super Bowl that past January.

It wasn't as if Joe was having a such a terrible season. He would finish the year ranked third in the league in passing, and his 27 touchdown passes were second only to Dan Marino's 30 as the NFL's best. Joe was even named the NFC starter in the Pro Bowl. And he was doing all that even while he was getting used to some new players, including a new rookie receiver named Jerry Rice.

The losses and the booing bothered Joe, but he knew that came with the territory when you're an NFL quarterback. What came next, however, really disturbed him. Sometime in November, rumors began circulating around the San Francisco area that Joe was using illegal drugs. One rumor had it that Joe had been arrested for speeding in his red Ferrari and that a controlled substance, which is a drug that is illegal unless a doctor has prescribed it, had been found in the car. Another rumor was that Joe had been admitted to a drug rehabilitation center.

The rumors were never proven to be true. They weren't even reported in the media until Joe and Coach Walsh issued public denials. "These are absurd, ridiculous, factless strings of gossip about a player, and it has affected Joe," Coach Walsh said at his weekly press conference on November 12, 1985. "I think it has been a very unfair thing. The team has not done well, Joe has not had a great season, and people are looking for explanations. And the juiciest would be that the great player is now at the mercy of a drug substance." But the rumors still persisted after this statement.

Despite the negative attention Joe was receiving, he continued to play hard during the 1985 season. The Los Angeles Rams had clinched the NFC West title, and the 49ers had to win their final two games of the regular season in order to earn a wild card spot in the playoffs. At that time, the playoffs in each conference were open only to the three division champions plus the two teams with the next best records, which were called the wild card teams. The 49ers beat the Saints in New Orleans, 31-19, and the Cowboys at Candlestick Park, 31-16, to finish the regular season. The 49ers were headed to New York for a playoff date against the New York Giants, the other wild card team. The Giants were known for their tough, hard-hitting defense.

During the week leading up to the Giants game, Joe was suffering from a pulled abdominal muscle. He also had a cold, and the combination of the two conditions caused him a lot of pain every time he coughed or sneezed. Joe didn't want to use pain killers, because he didn't like needles and was afraid of doing more damage if the pain were deadened. But with a playoff game coming up, Joe felt that he couldn't take the chance of not feeling his best. He received eight injections between Wednesday and game time on Sunday.

The pain killers didn't help, however, once the game began and Joe was hit on the shoulder by Giants linebacker Lawrence Taylor. Joe stayed in the game and completed 26 of 47 passes for 296 yards, but it wasn't enough. The Giants beat San Francisco 17-3 to end the 49ers' dream of repeating as Super Bowl champions.

For Joe it was the end of a long, painful season. "The next time you think you would like to leave what you're doing and trade it for the life of a high-profile athlete," Joe writes in his autobiography, "think twice."

9

Joe's Back!

Joe was happy to put the 1985 season behind him. He was looking forward to 1986. The 49ers had added several new players during the previous season, including nose guard Michael Carter, and now the newcomers were used to Coach Walsh's system.

Joe was beginning his eighth NFL season. He already was the highest-rated quarterback in NFL history, and he was only 30 years old. But the bad luck that had plagued Joe last season was still following him around.

In the third quarter of the 49ers' 1986 season opener against Tampa Bay, Joe was scrambling to his left on a pass play when he spotted an open receiver to his right. Hurrying to throw the pass, Joe twisted his body awkwardly in the air and felt a wrenching pain across his back.

Joe had been bothered by back problems all the previous season, but he ignored the pain and kept playing. It wasn't until later in the half, when a linebacker tossed him to the ground after an incomplete pass, that Joe left the game. The 49ers were well on their way to a 31-7 victory.

Joe had no idea how serious an injury he had suffered. But on the airplane ride home from Tampa, his back became very stiff. When he returned to San Francisco, he was examined by the team's doctors. The news was not good. Tests showed that he had a ruptured disk in his lower back.

A ruptured disk is a very painful injury. The disk is a rubbery material that acts as a cushion between the vertebrae in the spine. When the lowermost disk in the back ruptures, or tears, it can put pressure on the nerves leading to either leg, causing pain, numbness, and weakness in the leg.

Joe received an anti-inflammatory shot in his lower back to help ease the pain and swelling. He was then forced to stay home while strapped into a portable traction unit, which elevates the body into a more comfortable position by using weights and pulleys.

When the doctors examined him at the end of that week, the news was even worse. They told Joe that not only would he need surgery and miss the rest of the season, but he might never play football again.

It should have been crushing news for a great athlete who had played football since his days as a kid growing up in Monongahela and who was now at the top of his game. But Joe was still Joe Cool. A couple of days before the operation, Joe talked with his friend and teammate, Dwight Clark, about the operation. "He was very nervous, but he was confident," Dwight said at the time. The operation lasted two and a half hours. The doctors removed the torn part of Joe's disk by cutting a four-to-five inch opening in the spine above the injury and extracting the disk material with a spoon-like instrument.

The day after the operation, when Joe was moved from the recovery room into his own room at St. Mary's Hospital in San Francisco, Joe's parents were there, waiting. They had moved to the Bay Area that spring, after Mr. Montana retired, to be near Joe and their grandchild. Mrs. Montana remembers wanting to cry. "I thought he was finished," Mrs. Montana recalls. "They wheeled him in, sat him up, or at least tried to. I could see the pain in his eyes."

Joe's teammates Dwight Clark, Ronnie Lott, and Wendell Tyler also visited Joe at the hospital. After they saw him, they were sure he was never coming back to play pro football. "As soon as the doors closed," said Ronnie Lott, "Dwight and I looked at each other and both of us were thinking, 'It's no way. Ever.' It was scary, and really sad."

Joe's back operation was big news in San Francisco. On September 15, 1986, the lead story on the front page of each of the Bay Area's three major newspapers was that Joe would undergo surgery that day. The announcement was complete with charts and diagrams explaining Joe's condition and the operation.

After the operation, fans who had been calling for Joe's head just a year earlier, were now very worried about the health of his back. In order to accommodate all the phone requests for information about Joe, the hospital installed a Joe Montana hot line. A special telephone number was hooked into a recorded message that gave Joe's latest condition. The message said that Joe was progressing well and that he thanked everyone for their interest.

In the five days following Joe's operation, more than

10,000 people called the Joe Montana hot line. The 49ers received another 10,000 get-well cards for Joe. Joe also received hundreds of flower arrangements, stuffed animals, dolls, ornaments, balloons, ceramic footballs, T-shirts, and cassette tapes with music that he could work out to when he was feeling better.

Nobody thought Joe would be able to return to play for the 49ers that season. Maybe after a year or so of rehabilitation his back would be strong enough for him to play football again. But that was still a "maybe." Joe didn't need to rush himself back. He didn't need the money. If Joe had been forced to retire, he would have been eligible to receive $4.25 million, and most of it would have come from an insurance policy Joe had taken out with the Lloyd's of London insurance company. Many professional athletes take out such insurance policies so that they will still have an income if an injury ends their playing careers.

But giving up without a fight wasn't Joe's style. After all, hadn't his father taught him never to quit? Two days after the operation, Joe's mother asked her son: "What do you want to do?" Joe replied: "I want to play football again."

Joe was determined to come back and play as soon as

he possibly could. The day after surgery, while he was still connected to an intravenous tube that was feeding him medication, Joe walked for almost 10 minutes. Just three days after his operation, Joe did exercises. On the fourth day, he worked with light weights. On the fifth day, he walked for nearly 30 minutes and he began climbing stairs. On the seventh day, Joe walked a mile to and from rehabilitation.

On Monday, September 22, 1986, just one week after his operation, Joe was released from the hospital. At that point, some of the doctors, after seeing how determined Joe was, had changed their minds about his comeback attempt. Dr. Arthur White, who had operated on Joe, said that Joe should be able to play football again in two to three months. However, Coach Walsh wasn't planning on miracles. He said he didn't expect Joe back until the following season. He planned on using reserve quarterback Jeff Kemp for the remainder of the season.

About a week after he returned home, Joe said he was going to try to come back before the end of the 1986 season. He worked hard to rehabilitate himself as quickly as possible. He worked on weight-training equipment to re-strengthen his stomach and back muscles and he increased his walking to twice a day, a 30-minute walk and a 20-minute walk.

By the third week after his operation, Joe was jogging and swimming. He even began doing staggered, broken-field type running. Going through rehabilitation can be painful and tedious, but Joe was a dedicated patient.

On October 13, less than a month after his operation, Joe threw a football for 15 minutes at the 49ers training camp. That week, Joe rejoined the team in practice. He ran the second and third units. And it was just one month before that a doctor had said Joe might never play football again.

One of the drills Joe went through during his rehabilitation was the sock drill, which was used instead of wind sprints. Jerry Attaway, the 49ers physical development coordinator, threw socks that were weighted with lead. Joe would take a deep drop on the practice field, and a sock would be pitched 5 or 15 yards to his left or right. Joe would sprint over to where the sock dropped and set up to pass. Then, another sock would immediately be pitched the other way. Joe would twist, spin, race over, and set up again and again during the 10-minute drill. "The sock drill was the worst, the very worst," Joe remembers.

Joe's rehabilitation kept moving along, much faster than anyone anticipated. During the last two weeks of October, Joe worked out with the 49ers in full pads, but he still didn't take part in any contact drills. Joe's really big day came on November 3rd. With Dr. White looking on, Joe worked out with the 49ers starting unit for the first time.

Dr. White said that even though Joe's rehabilitation "has been the fastest recovery I have ever seen in any individual I have operated on," he was concerned about Joe reinjuring his back. He thought it would be wise if Joe did not return to professional football. Still, Dr. White gave Joe medical clearance to play.

The next day Coach Walsh announced that Joe would most likely be his starting quarterback against St. Louis that Sunday. The 49ers' record while Joe had been out was a disappointing 4-3 with 1 tie against Atlanta. Coach Walsh was hopeful that Joe would inspire the team to play better in the second half of the season. Just 55 days after his operation and just eight games after he was hurt against Tampa Bay, Joe came back. When he was introduced before the game against the St. Louis Cardinals, Joe was greeted by a standing ovation from the 59,172 fans at Candlestick Park. The field was surrounded with banners saying: WELCOME BACK, JOE, WE LOVE YOU and WAY TO GO JOE.

"An electric chill went through the whole team when Montana was introduced," said former 49ers safety Tom Holmoe after the game.

Once Joe was back on the field, he was his old self. Wearing a heavily-padded flak jacket under his jersey to protect his body against a hard hit, Joe completed 13 of 19 passes for 270 yards and three touchdowns. The 49ers won the game 43-17. For the first time in his pro career, Joe threw three long touchdown passes in one game!

"I knew he'd be good," said Dwight Clark that day. "I knew he'd inspire us. But I didn't think he'd come back after two months and be right on the money."

Joe admitted that he was a little nervous before the game, but that was gone after Cardinals linebacker Charlie Baker decked him on a blitz in the first quarter. The crowd and his teammates gasped when Joe went down, but Joe said he was happy to get that first hit over with. "I was glad to get it out of my mind," he said. "If you are afraid of getting hit, or hurt, then you are going to get hurt." Joe got hit eight times, but he didn't get hurt. He showed that he could still move in and out of the pocket and that he could still throw on the run.

Joe earned the respect of his opponents as well as his teammates. During the second quarter of the game, St. Louis defensive end Al Baker hit Joe as Joe released a long pass to Jerry Rice. Baker was still sitting on Joe as they both watched Rice turn the pass into a 40-yard touchdown. Said Baker to Joe after the play: "You're a heckuva man."

Joe led the 49ers into the playoffs with five wins in their final seven regular season games. In the eight regular season games he played in that season, including the first game of the season when he got hurt, Joe completed 62 percent of his passes for 2,236 yards and eight touchdowns. But even with his amazing comeback, Joe was still not satisfied. "When I came back, it felt like I had sat out a year," Joe recalls. "Sometimes I thought I played well. Sometimes I didn't. I was disappointed that I wasn't quite as sharp as I had been."

The 49ers won their fourth NFC West title since 1981. The day after the last game of the season, on December 20, Joe got an even better prize when Jennifer Montana gave birth to a daughter, Elizabeth. Then, for the second season in a row, he and the 49ers traveled East to face the Giants in a playoff game at Giants Stadium.

And for the second season in a row, the Giants eliminated the 49ers. This time, it was a 49-3 rout. The Giants were on their way to becoming Super Bowl champions.

Joe was knocked out of the game in the second quarter when noseguard Jim Burt, who later became a 49er, crashed into him as he released the ball. Joe was knocked out cold. He had suffered a concussion and spent the night in the hospital for observation. His back, however, was fine.

It was certainly not the way Joe wanted to end his season. But then, after his injury, who ever expected to see Joe Montana on a football field that January. He was the Comeback Kid in more ways than one.

10

Benched

Just one year after doctors said he might never play football again, Joe was playing, in the words of Coach Walsh, "at his very best."

The 1987 regular season was a great one for both Joe and the 49ers. The team won 13 games and lost only 2. In a game against Green Bay, Joe completed his first 17 passes, giving him a league-record 22 straight over two games. Joe was the NFL's top-rated passer for the first time in his career and he threw for a club record and league-leading 31 touchdowns. And those 31 TD passes were worth even more because Joe donated $200 for each one (for a total of $6200) to the Crippled Children's Society of Santa Clara County.

The play of the 49ers, and especially Joe's performance, was even more remarkable considering two things. One was that the team was once again torn apart by a strike by the NFL Players Association (NFLPA). Because of the strike, one game was canceled and three others were played with "replacement" players instead of the regular team members. Replacement players were players who had not been good enough to make an NFL team. They had been working at other jobs, staying in shape and waiting for their shot at the big time. They did not belong to the union.

The NFLPA called the strike to try to force the team owners to allow players to become free agents after their contracts expired, just like in baseball and basketball. Although the players now all wanted free agency, they were divided over whether a strike was the best way to get the job done. Joe, who had quit the players' union just before the last strike, honored the strike at first, but then was one of 17 49ers who crossed the picket line. Initially, he was concerned about other players who were not being paid as well as he was. But even though Joe was making a lot of money, he finally decided he couldn't afford to lose the money that would be deducted from his salary if he stayed out on strike.

Friendships and team unity were strained by the split among the 49ers during the three-week strike. When the strike ended, the veterans remembered the hard feelings that had hurt the team after the last strike and were determined not to let that happen again. "I told the guys not to look at the small picture," said 49ers safety Ronnie Lott. "That if we held the last three weeks against each other — after all we'd lived through — we'd be pretty shallow people."

The second thing that made the season so remarkable was that Joe passed for 31 touchdowns even though he missed most of the last three regular season games with an injury. In the first quarter of a game against the Bears, Joe pulled a hamstring muscle, which is the long muscle that runs down the back of the leg, and had to leave the game. With reserve quarterback Steve Young filling in, the 49ers defeated the Bears 41-0.

The 49ers had already clinched a playoff spot, so there was no need to rush Joe back into action. While Joe rested for the playoffs, Steve stayed at the controls the following week when the 49ers beat the Atlanta Falcons 35-7, and the week after that when San Francisco stomped on the Los Angeles Rams, 48-0.

It was an impressive job by Steve Young, whom the 49ers had acquired from the Tampa Bay Buccaneers in April. Steve had been a star quarterback in college at Brigham Young University, the school named in honor of his great-great-great grandfather. After college, Steve signed an incredible $42 million contract with the Los Angeles Express of the United States Football League (which is now out of business). After playing two seasons with the Express and two seasons with the Buccaneers, he was traded to the 49ers.

Joe came back in time for the playoffs. And after such a dominating finish, the 49ers were heavy favorites against Minnesota in their opening playoff game at home. Yet, on a rain-soaked field at Candlestick Park, the Vikings shocked the 49ers. Minnesota jumped out to a 20-3 lead midway through the second quarter when defensive back Reggie Rutland intercepted Joe's pass and returned it 45 yards for a touchdown. The Minnesota defense smothered the 49ers and Joe, who, because of the constant pressure, had nowhere to throw. Joe completed only 12 of 26 passes for 109 yards.

With 6:29 to play in the third quarter and the 49ers trailing 27-10, Coach Walsh did the unthinkable. He benched Joe and brought in Steve Young. It was the first time Coach Walsh had ever benched Joe. And it was the first time Joe had ever been benched. "Getting pulled was real tough, but the hardest part was, after one game, people were talking like I was being judged on a bad year," Joe said later. "I was being judged on one game."

With Steve at quarterback, the 49ers were able to make the score a lot closer. But the Vikings won the game, 36-24, and knocked San Francisco out of the playoffs. It was a major disappointment for the team and its followers, who were expecting another Super Bowl victory after such a strong regular season.

Fans and members of the media began to wonder if the 49ers were going to make a change at quarterback. During the off-season, there was talk of the 49ers possibly trading Joe and going with Steve Young as the starting quarterback.

Coach Walsh was opposed to getting rid of Joe in favor of Steve. He felt that Joe still had plenty of good seasons left in him. But 49ers owner Edward DeBartolo, Junior, was so upset with the team's loss to the Minnesota Vikings that he thought a change in personnel might be needed. Steve was 26 years old, Joe was 32. And Steve was the type of quarterback who could do well in Coach Walsh's offense because, like Joe, Steve knew how to move out of the pocket and he could throw on the run.

After every season, the NFL team owners, coaches, and general managers hold meetings to talk about business. At the NFL meetings in Phoenix, Arizona, following the 1987 season, DeBartolo told his fellow owners that he would trade Joe if the price was right.

Joe wasn't pleased with the trade talk and he wanted to stay with the 49ers, but he realized that trades are a part of the business. He also knew that the decision was out of his hands. All he could do was get himself ready for the next season — wherever he would be playing.

First, Joe had to undergo minor surgery for a sore right elbow that had bothered him at times during the season. Once that was done, Joe geared himself up for another challenge. He was determined to get into the best shape of his professional career. Joe had missed parts of the past five seasons with injuries. He wanted to be able to stay healthy for an entire season.

Working with fitness expert Ben Parks three days a week, Joe would get up at 5:30 in the morning to run, work with weights, shadow box, and do aerobics. By weightlifting and changing his diet, he purposely increased his weight from 185 to 198 pounds so that he would be stronger over the long NFL season.

When training camp began, Joe said, "Physically, I'm probably in better shape than I've been in a long time."

Joe played brilliantly during the exhibition season. He was determined to give Coach Walsh no choice but to keep him as the 49ers starting quarterback when the regular season began. In one exhibition game, Joe completed 12 of 14 passes for 166 yards just in the first half!

In the season opener, a 34-33 victory over New Orleans, Joe started at quarterback and threw three third-quarter touchdown passes. But then Joe suffered a bruised elbow on his throwing arm and had to leave the game.

During the week leading up to the 49ers' next game, against the New York Giants on Monday night, Steve Young worked with the first team in practice for two days. It appeared to Joe that Coach Walsh was no longer sure about who the starter should be and was playing musical quarterbacks with Joe and Steve.

The next week against the New York Giants, Steve

Young started at quarterback. But with the 49ers trailing at the start of the second half, Joe came off the bench to take over. Even at age 32, Joe showed he was still the Comeback Kid when he connected with Jerry Rice on a 78-yard touchdown play with just 42 seconds on the clock to give the 49ers a 20-17 win.

Joe and Steve continued to take turns at quarterback during the rest of the season. Steve started three games and replaced Joe in eight other games when Coach Walsh removed Joe from the field because of injuries to Joe's back, knees, ribs, and elbow. Once Coach Walsh pulled Joe because Joe was suffering from a bad case of the flu. Despite Joe's off-season training program, he was still bothered by numerous ailments.

Coach Walsh said he had to rest Joe because he felt Joe was physically worn down for much of the season. Joe, who didn't usually ask to leave a game even when he was hurt, felt that since he had played with nagging injuries throughout other seasons, there was no reason for Coach Walsh to keep pulling him now. He wondered whether Coach Walsh was using the injuries as an excuse to pull him from the game.

Normally confident Joe was now hesitant to try certain passes because he was afraid that a mistake would result in his being benched. "You're a little more tentative and you tend to aim a little bit and say, 'I hope it gets there because I know if it doesn't, I might not be in here,'" Joe said.

Joe knew he wasn't through as an NFL quarterback, but he was wondering whether he might have to go to another team to prove it.

Once, earlier in the season, Joe and Coach Walsh had a heart-to-heart talk about Joe's unhappiness. Joe left the meeting and, determined to prove himself on the field, went out that week and completed 20 of 29 passes for 302 yards and four touchdown passes in a 38-7 win over the Seattle Seahawks. But it wasn't until late in the season, when the 49ers were 6-5 and not headed for the playoffs, that Coach Walsh finally decided once and for all that he needed Joe as his number 1 quarterback. He turned the starting job over to Joe and asked him to perform his magic.

Joe responded like a champion who knows how to win the big games. He led the 49ers to four straight victories — knocking off the Redskins, the Chargers, the Falcons, and the Saints. The 49ers won their third consecutive NFC West title. And they were just getting warmed up.

In the playoffs, Joe and the 49ers reached their peak. In the opening game, Joe threw three touchdown passes to Jerry Rice in a 34-9 win over Minnesota to avenge the playoff loss of a year ago. The next week, in the NFC Championship game against the Chicago Bears at Soldier Field, the temperature at the opening kickoff, with the wind-chill factor, felt like 26 degrees below zero. Joe wore a glove on his left hand and put his right hand into the pocket of his jersey between plays. Despite the weather conditions, Joe completed 17 of 27 passes for 288 yards and three touchdowns with no interceptions. Two of the touchdowns were to Joe's favorite receiver, Jerry Rice.

But Joe saved his most dramatic performance for the Super Bowl when he completed "The Drive" to lead the 49ers to a thrilling come-from-behind 20-16 win over the Cincinnati Bengals with only 34 seconds left.

Jerry Rice was named MVP of that game, but Joe didn't mind. He didn't need a trophy for people to know who was the number 1 quarterback on the 49ers.

11

Dream Season

That spring, after the 49ers' Super Bowl win over Cincinnati, Joe and the team doctors decided that Joe should have surgery on his left knee, which had been giving him trouble on and off during the previous few seasons.

Because of all the banging they take on the field, football players have to accept injuries and surgery as a fact of life. The knee is a particularly sensitive area for a quarterback because of all the twisting and turning he must do. This was Joe's fifth operation since 1983 and his second on that same knee.

But by the time training camp opened, Joe was feeling great. He and Jennifer were expecting their third child sometime early in the season. A son, Nathaniel Joseph Montana, would be born on October 3, 1989. In his 10th season with the 49ers, Joe was also facing a new challenge that helped get his adrenaline flowing: Could the 49ers repeat as Super Bowl champions with a new head coach?

Following the team's dramatic 20-16 Super Bowl win over Cincinnati, Coach Bill Walsh decided to retire from coaching and go into broadcasting. He became a commentator on pro football games for NBC. Coach Walsh was replaced as head coach by George Seifert, who had been the 49ers defensive coordinator.

Coach Seifert was already respected by the players. As defensive coordinator, he had been the assistant coach in charge of the defensive players and he had helped make them into one of the league's finest units. In the 1988 season, the 49ers defense was third in the NFL (out of 28 teams) in total defense, which is measured by how many total yards a team allows opposing offenses to gain. Fewer is better. In 1987 the 49ers were ranked number 1 in the league in total defense!

Like Bill Walsh, Coach Seifert was a soft-spoken, quiet man with a low-key personality. He knew that he didn't want to start off his first season as head coach with another quarterback controversy like the team had had the year before. So one of Coach Seifert's first acts was to announce that Joe was going to be the team's starting quarterback.

But George Seifert was unlike Bill Walsh in one major way. He was an expert on defense, not offense. Yet he knew what he didn't know, so another one of his first moves was to promote Mike Holmgren from quarterback coach to offensive coordinator, in charge of the entire offense. Coach Seifert knew that to make the 49ers offense go, he would have to rely on Coach Holmgren and Joe.

Mike Holmgren had worked with the 49ers quarterbacks for three seasons and had helped Joe win his first NFL passing title in 1987. Coach Walsh used to take care of the team's play calling and play designing. Now Coach Holmgren would have that responsibility. Coach Holmgren already had some ideas for Joe. He wanted to take better advantage of Joe's great talent to read defenses and change plays after he saw how the defensive team was lined up. He also wanted Joe to continue rolling out to give the receivers more time to get open. But Coach Holmgren also felt there were some things Joe could do differently.

From studying game films, Coach Holmgren had learned that Joe still had a tendency to try to throw a pass to a receiver even if the receiver was well covered by a defensive player. He wanted Joe to throw the pass away rather than try to force it. He also wanted Joe to take three steps back instead of seven steps when he dropped back from the line of scrimmage to pass. This way Joe would get rid of the ball more quickly, before the defense was ready, and there would be a better chance the pass would be completed.

Coach Holmgren also wanted Joe to throw more passes to two offensive players who had seldom been his targets. With defenses trying to stop Joe's favorite receiver, Jerry Rice, Coach Holmgren wanted Joe to throw the ball to fullback Tom Rathman or wide receiver John Taylor.

It is to Joe's credit that after all his years of success he was still willing to take advice and learn new things from a new coach. First of all, Joe felt more relaxed under his new coaches. He also felt that the changes that Coaches Seifert and Holmgren had made had revitalized him by forcing him to study his playbook more and concentrate more in practice.

Still, with the team getting used to a new coach, the season began a little shakily. First, there was a nail-biter of a win over Indianapolis, 30-24. In the second game of the season, against Tampa Bay, Joe became the "Comeback Kid" again when he drove the 49ers 70 yards in 10 plays and scored the winning touchdown on a four-yard run with 40 seconds to play. The 49ers won 20-16.

The next week, Joe pulled out a 38-28 victory over the Philadelphia Eagles after the 49ers trailed by 11 points with 13 minutes, 40 seconds to play. In the final 13 minutes, Joe — who had been sacked seven times and was suffering from bruised ribs — threw touchdown passes of 70, 8, 24, and 33 yards to four different receivers. Four touchdown passes in one quarter was a new 49ers record.

All in all, Joe directed five fourth-quarter rallies in the 1989 season! And as the offense became accustomed to Coach Holmgren's game plan, the 49ers began to roll. After losing the fourth game of the season to the Rams 13-12, the 49ers won their next six straight before falling to the Packers 21-17. Then they won their next five games, capping off the season with a 26-0 shutout of the Chicago Bears. They won the NFC Western Division title with a 14-2 record.

Joe passed for 3,521 yards during the season. This marked the sixth time that he had passed for more than 3,000 yards in a season, tying former San Diego Charger quarterback Dan Fouts' league record. Following Coach Holmgren's advice about not forcing the pass, Joe threw 154 consecutive passes without an interception. Fullback Tom Rathman and wide receiver John Taylor, who combined for 56 catches in 1988, became an integral part of the offense. In 1989 they caught 113 passes. The 49er offense led the NFL in total yards gained by passing and running.

Joe had the highest single-season quarterback rating in NFL history (112.4), surpassing the previous all-time high of 110.4 by Cleveland Browns quarterback Milt Plum in 1960. And Joe had the third-highest completion percentage (70.2) in history. It was without a doubt Joe's greatest season. Based on the NFL quarterback rating system, it was the best season any NFL quarterback has ever had!

Joe's incredible season did not go unnoticed. After the season, Joe would be named the Player of the Year by *Sports Illustrated* and the Man of the Year by *The Sporting News*. And in a vote by members of the NFL Players Association, Joe would win the Jim Thorpe Trophy as the most valuable player. For the second time in his career, Joe would be selected by his teammates as winner of the Len Eshmont

Award, given annually to the individual who exhibits courageous and inspirational play. And for the first time in his career, he would be named Most Valuable Player for the season by the Associated Press. All of these honors are based upon a player's regular season performance but they are not awarded until after the playoffs.

And Joe's season wasn't over yet. The playoffs were ready to begin. Inside his locker at Candlestick Park, Joe had hung a photograph of his three children — Alexandra, 4; Elizabeth, 3; and Nathaniel, just 3 months — each holding a Super Bowl ring. Underneath the photo, there was taped a caption: "Okay, Daddy, next ring is yours."

As dominant as Joe and the 49ers were throughout the regular season, they were even more dominant during the playoffs. The 49ers showed how tough they could be when they demolished the Minnesota Vikings 41-13 in the opening round of the playoffs. In the first half alone, Joe completed 13 of 16 passes for 210 yards and four touchdowns to give the 49ers a 27-3 lead.

In the NFC championship game against the Los Angeles Rams, the Rams scored first on a field goal, but then it was all San Francisco. This game was also all but over after the last drive in the first half. The 49ers had the ball on their own 17-yard line with only two minutes left in the half. Then, incredibly, they ran eight plays in 111 seconds with Joe throwing all kinds of quick passes. Finally, with the ball on the Rams 18-yard line and nine seconds left, Joe waited behind the protection of his offensive linemen while wide receiver John Taylor faked Rams cornerback LeRoy Irvin three different ways before Joe hit him with a touchdown pass. That made the score 21-3.

When it was all over, Joe had completed 26 of 30 passes for 262 yards and two touchdowns in a 30-3 victory. He only threw four incomplete passes all game, and two of the four he threw away on purpose.

Joe's six touchdown passes in the playoffs gave him an NFL record 31 career postseason touchdown passes, surpassing the previous mark of 30 held by Pittsburgh Steelers great Terry Bradshaw.

The records and awards were great, but what made Joe happiest was that the 49ers were headed back to the Super Bowl. They would have a chance to win back-to-back Super Bowls. San Francisco was going to face the Denver Broncos in Super Bowl XXIV at the Superdome in New Orleans,

Louisiana. It would be 33-year-old Joe Montana (3-0 in previous Super Bowls) against 29-year-old star quarterback John Elway (0-2 in Super Bowls).

The 49ers were heavy favorites against Denver, but there was one statistic in the Broncos' favor. The Broncos were the only team the 49ers did not beat in the 1980s. Denver was 3-0 against San Francisco, beating them by a total of seven points in the three games.

As it turned out, that statistic was meaningless on January 28, 1990. Once the game began, it was never close. There were records breaking all over the place. Joe completed 22 of 29 passes for 297 yards and he threw for a Super Bowl record five touchdowns. He connected on a Super Bowl record 13 consecutive passes in one stretch between the second and third quarters. Joe's primary receiver was Jerry Rice, as he had been throughout the season. Jerry caught seven passes for 148 yards and a Super Bowl record three touchdowns. The 49ers scored more points than any team had ever scored in a Super Bowl. Their 55-10 victory was the most one-sided Super Bowl ever played.

Joe won his record third Super Bowl Most Valuable Player trophy and he joined former Steelers quarterback

Terry Bradshaw as the only quarterbacks to lead their teams to four Super Bowl victories. It certainly was a record-setting day for Joe and the 49ers. Joe's 11 Super Bowl touchdowns set a career mark and his total of 1,142 yards passing topped Terry Bradshaw's previous record of 932 yards. Incredibly, Joe had thrown 122 passes in four Super Bowls without one interception. In appreciation for the great protection they gave him all season, Joe presented all of his linemen with gold Rolex Presidential watches.

When Joe was asked to compare his four Super Bowl championship teams, he said: "It's hard to take any team above this one, offensively or defensively. I think we put everything together."

The 49ers became the first NFL team to win back-to-back Super Bowls since the Pittsburgh Steelers did it in 1979 and 1980. They were also the first NFL franchise to win consecutive championships under two different head coaches. On top of that, George Seifert became only the second rookie head coach ever to win the Super Bowl.

The San Francisco 49ers had proven that they were the team of the 1980s and Joe Montana had proven that he was the quarterback of the decade.

12

The Greatest QB Ever?

When 49ers Coach George Seifert was asked to sum up Joe's career, following his team's victory in the 1990 Super Bowl, he said it all in a simple sentence: "He's probably the greatest quarterback to play the game."

Because of Joe's great success, coaches, players, and sportswriters alike have begun comparing him to some of the all-time greats who played quarterback in the NFL. Before the 1990 Super Bowl, columnist Dave Anderson of *The New York Times* asked a Hall of Fame lineup of former quarterbacks to evaluate Joe's place in history. They were unanimous in their opinion.

"Joe is so consistently outstanding, he belongs up there

at the top of the class," said former Pittsburgh Steelers quarterback Terry Bradshaw.

"Overall, Joe Montana has played the position better than anybody else ever has," said former Dallas Cowboys quarterback Roger Staubach.

"I don't think you can go wrong saying Montana is the best quarterback in history," said former New York Jets quarterback Joe Namath.

"I think Montana's the best ever," said former Green Bay Packers quarterback Bart Starr, who led the Packers to five NFL championships, including their first two Super Bowls.

Joe's record backs up these opinions. Going into the 1990 season, Joe ranked as the NFL's all-time leader in overall passing efficiency and completion percentage. He was third in career pass completions, fifth in passing yardage, and sixth in touchdown passes. He has set an NFL record by passing for over 3,000 yards in a season six times, and holds the playoff records for most passes attempted and most completions in a career. He also holds the Super Bowl records for most passes completed, highest completion percentage, most yards gained in a game, and most attempts without an interception in a game.

It could have gone to Joe's head — being more success-ful than the players he grew up idolizing. But Joe doesn't feel comfortable talking about himself that way. "Those things are reserved for guys who are no longer in the game," he says.

Instead, Joe continues to let his play on the field speak for itself. Once the 1990 season started, Joe picked up where he left off the season before. It was a year full of highlights.

In the first game of the year, against the New Orleans Saints on a Monday night, Joe and the 49ers were trailing 12-10 with just over nine minutes left to play in the game and no time-outs remaining. The Saints defense had been brutal, and Joe had been sacked six times. But this was clutch time, Joe's time to shine.

The Saints defense, afraid of the 49ers completing a long pass, backed off a little and Joe took advantage. The Comeback Kid found John Taylor free for a 25-yard gain, and Jerry Rice for 20 yards. That set up a field goal by 49er kicker Mike Cofer with just nine seconds to play. The 49ers won 13-12.

The next week, Joe became the 49ers' career leader in

passing yardage as he completed 29 of 44 passes for 390 yards in a 26-13 win over the Washington Redskins. With that performance, Joe surpassed the San Francisco record of 31,548 yards set by John Brodie, who played for the 49ers from 1957 to 1973.

In the fifth game of the season, against Atlanta, the Falcons tried a different defensive plan to try and stop Joe. The Falcon defense used an all-out, nonstop blitz all game, trying to sack Joe before he could throw the ball. But Joe countered like a smart boxer fighting a wild-swinging slugger, by throwing short quick passes to his receivers before he could be sacked. Joe completed 32 of 49 passes for a 49ers record 476 yards and six touchdowns in their 45-35 win.

Joe kept right on rolling. The 49ers won their first 10 games before losing to the Rams, 28-17. The next week, they went head to head against the New York Giants, who were also 10-1, at Candlestick Park, and defeated them in a defensive battle, 7-3. The 49ers lost only once more during the regular season, to the New Orleans Saints by a score of 13-10. The 49ers completed the 1990 regular season with a league-best 14-2 record and Joe was named the NFL Most Valuable Player for the second year in a row by the Associated Press. Joe's successful season reached its peak when *Sports Illustrated* named him "Sportsman of the Year" for 1990. He was the first pro football player to win the award outright in the magazine's 37 years.

With the best regular season record in the league, Joe and the 49ers were once again in the playoffs, this time trying to win their third Super Bowl in a row — to "three-peat" as the fans and newspaper headline writers liked to say. No team in NFL history had ever won three consecutive Super Bowls.

The playoffs started on a promising note. In the semi-final game, the 49ers roared past the Washington Redskins 28-10. Joe completed 22 of his 31 pass attempts for 274 yards and two touchdowns. Joe was good but he was not perfect. He threw his first interception after 180 consecutive completions in post-season play. It was a cool, efficient performance.

The following week was the NFC Championship Game, and standing between the 49ers and their dream of a third consecutive Super Bowl were the always-dangerous New York Giants. The game turned out to be a real cliff-hanger, but Joe and the 49ers seemed to be in control.

Then with the 49ers holding the ball and leading 13-12 in the fourth quarter, Joe dropped back to pass. As he waited for a receiver to get open, he didn't see Giants lineman Leonard Marshall barreling in on him from the other side. Marshall sacked Joe so hard that the ball squirted out of Joe's hands and sailed nine yards before the 49ers recovered. Joe stayed down on the turf after the play was over, with a broken finger on his throwing hand and a bruised breastbone. Even if the 49ers could win this game, Joe's season was over.

But as it turned out, without Joe, the 49ers' season was over, too. The Giants won the game in a dramatic comeback of their own. They recovered a 49ers fumble, then drove slowly down the field, using up time on the clock. Finally, with just three seconds left, they kicked a field goal to win the game, 15-13. New York, which would go on to beat the Buffalo Bills in the Super Bowl, had discovered the only way to stop Joe Montana from coming from behind to win a game is to keep him off the field until the game is over.

Joe has certainly come a long way since he was that 8-year-old back in Monongahela throwing spirals to his dad in the neighbors' backyard. But that quiet self-confidence that he developed back then helped him get past the bumps and potholes on his road to the top of the NFL.

When his high school coach and college coach failed to see how special his talents were and made him sit on the bench, Joe kept on working and practicing, waiting for his chance. When the 49ers drafted him and Coach Walsh gave him the chance to be the starter, Joe studied the plays until he knew them as well as his coaches did. When a back injury threatened to end his career, Joe decided that he would return to the team that season, and did everything he could to make it happen. When he was criticized by the fans and the media, and benched by his coach, Joe kept his head up and worked harder than he ever had before.

Joe is enjoying his success. He relishes the six months of vacation that playing pro football allows him, and during the off-season, he is rarely seen without his wife and three children.

He and his family can certainly afford a wonderful lifestyle. Shortly after the 49ers defeated the Broncos in the 1990 Super Bowl, Joe signed a three-year contract estimated to be worth between $3 million and $5 million to become a spokesman for the sneaker company, L.A. Gear. Soon after that, Joe and the 49ers agreed to a four-year contract, worth approximately $13 million, that made Joe the highest-paid player in the NFL.

Joe has paid the price in aching knees, stiff backs, sore shoulders, and bruised elbows. He is not going to push his son, Nathaniel, into football. After all the injuries Joe has had, he says he would prefer Nathaniel become something like a concert pianist instead of a football player.

After a game, you'll often find Joe sitting at his locker after everyone else leaves, with ice taped on his right elbow. He'll sometimes have trouble getting out of bed on the Monday morning after a tough game, the cost of taking a hit to complete a pass. And even at age 34, Joe's still as intense about the game as he was when he was a little boy. It's that quality that makes him Joe Montana.

In a poll of 14,000 readers conducted by *USA Today*, Joe was selected as the sports star that fans would most like to be. Those people probably didn't think about the difficult times Joe has had to endure along with the great days he's had since he was that skinny kid in Monongahela, Pennsylvania. But it is the combination of all those things that makes Joe Montana the sports legend he is today.

Joe's NFL Statistics

Year	G/S	Att.	Comp.	Yds.	Pct.	Int.	Long	TD	NFL Rating
1990	15/15	520	321	3944	.617	16	78t	26	89.0
1989	13/13	386	271	3521	.702	8	95t	26	112.4
1988	14/13	397	238	2981	.599	10	96t	18	87.9
1987	13/11	398	266	3054	.668	13	57t	31	102.1
1986	8/8	307	191	2236	.622	9	48	8	80.7
1985	15/15	494	303	3653	.613	13	66t	27	91.3
1984	16/15	432	279	3630	.646	10	80t	28	102.9
1983	16/16	515	332	3910	.645	12	77	26	94.6
1982	9/9	346	213	2613	.616	11	55	17	87.9
1981	16/16	488	311	3565	.637	12	58t	19	88.2
1980	15/7	273	176	1795	.645	9	71t	15	87.8
1979	16/1	23	13	96	.565	0	18	1	80.9

Football Field

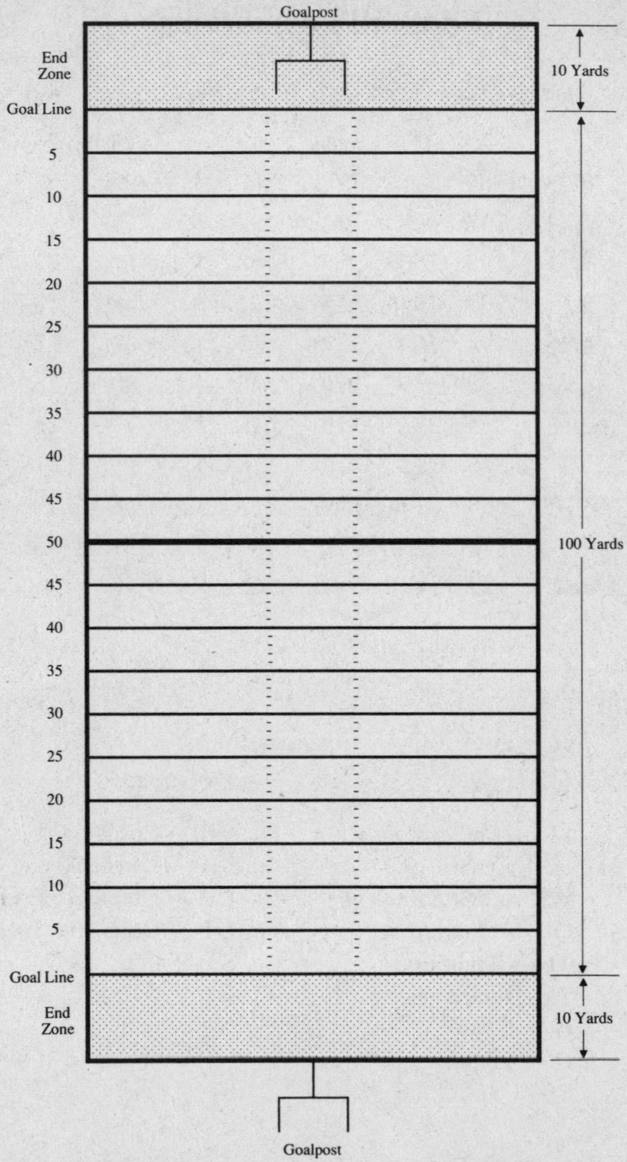

Goalpost

End Zone

10 Yards

Goal Line

5

10

15

20

25

30

35

40

45

50

100 Yards

45

40

35

30

25

20

15

10

5

Goal Line

End Zone

10 Yards

Goalpost

118

Football Formations

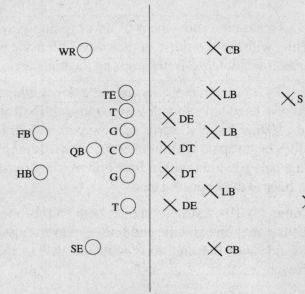

Line of Scrimmage

Offense

FB — Fullback
HB — Halfback
WR — Wide Receiver
QB — Quarterback
TE — Tight End
T — Tackle
G — Guard
C — Center
SE — Split End

Defense

CB — Cornerback
LB — Linebacker
DE — Defensive End
DT — Defensive Tackle
S — Safety

Glossary

Block: To stop the movement of an opposing player by hitting him with the shoulders or the body. Offensive blocking prevents the defense from reaching the ball carrier.

Down: Each offensive play is termed a down. Players on the offensive team have four downs to move the ball at least 10 yards. If they make 10 yards or more before their fourth down, they begin again with another first down. If they don't move the ball 10 yards within four downs, they must turn the ball over to the opposing team.

End Zone: A 10-yard-deep area at both ends of the field between the goal line and the end line. A player must cross the goal line into the end zone with the ball to make a touchdown.

Extra Point: After a touchdown, there is a chance for the scoring team to make an additional point by placekicking, passing, or running the ball into the end zone.

Forward Pass: A forward throw from the quarterback to a receiver.

Fumble: When a ball carrier drops the ball. The ball is still in play after a fumble and either team may recover the ball.

Goal Line: A line that stretches the width of the field, marking the beginning of the end zone. A player must carry or catch the ball behind this line in order to score a touchdown.

Kicking:

- **Placekick** – A kick in which the ball is held on the ground or placed in a kicking tee and then kicked. Often used for kickoffs, field goals, and extra point attempts.
- **Punt** – A kick in which the ball is dropped from the hands and is kicked before the ball reaches the ground. This is usually done when the offensive team has a fourth down.

Lateral Pass: When the ball is thrown parallel to the line of scrimmage or away from the offensive goal line.

Line of Scrimmage: An imaginary line parallel to the goal lines that marks the spot to which the ball was carried on the last play. The offense starts the next play from this line.

Rushing: The act of moving forward toward the end zone by running with the ball.

Sack: To tackle the opposing quarterback behind the line of scrimmage before he can pass the ball.

Scoring:

- **Field Goal** – A score of three points made by placekicking the ball through the goalposts and over the crossbar.
- **Point After** – After a touchdown is scored, the team has the opportunity to score an extra point. The team lines up on the 2 1/2 yard line, and the center snaps the ball to the holder, who sets up the ball for the placekicker. The kicker tries to kick the ball between the goalposts and over the crossbar. It is worth one point.

•Safety – When a member of the offensive team is tackled with the football in his own end zone, it is worth two points for the defense.

•Touchdown – A score of six points that is made by carrying the ball or completing a pass over an opponent's goal line.

Tackle: To throw or knock the ballcarrier to the ground, stopping him from going forward.